Kimberly

The Smokin' "HOT" Bride of Christ

"Exchanging Regrets
For Rewards
Before He Returns"

With Love,

Rosemary Fisher

Rosemary

The Smokin' "HOT" Bride of Christ
Published by Fisher Publishing
PO Box 535
Columbia, TN 38402

Italics, bold, brackets in Scripture quotations reflect the author's added emphasis. Brackets in all Scripture versions except those marked (AMP) are the author's parenthetical insertions.

ISBN- 1511489294

ISBN-13:978-1511489294

Printed in the United States of America

2014 First Edition

This book is available in special quantity discounts when purchased in bulk by corporations, organizations and special-interest groups. Custom imprinting or excerpting can also be done to fit special needs. For information and pricing, please email rosemary@rosemaryfisher.com.

DEDICATION

I dedicate this book to our son…
Beau Fisher

God has blessed you greatly!
You're faithful, loyal and sincere.
You're strong, witty and courageous.
You are a gift that your father and I cherish.
It has brought us great pleasure to raise and call you our Son.
I'll love you forever…

CONTENTS

INTRODUCTION   5 - 6

Chapter 1 - **Smokin' "HOT" or "NOT"?**   7 - 24

Chapter 2 - **Time to Repair, Renovate or Rebuild**   25 - 26

Special Bonus - Smokin' "Hot" to "Rapture Ready"[i]

Chapter 3 – **Does Anybody See Her**   28 - 32

Chapter 4 – **It's Only a Book**   33 - 37

Chapter 5 – **Life Beyond Regret**   38 - 44

Chapter 6 – **The Modern Woman at the Well**   45 - 50

Chapter 7 – **The God Who Laughed at my Jokes**   51 - 66

Chapter 8 – **Witchcraft to God's Warrior**   67 - 73

Chapter 9 - **Unconditional Love**   74 – 82

Chapter 10 – **Commitment To Christ**   83 - 85

The Bride of Christ Rapture Ready Bible Study

Day 1 – **A Virgin Bride**   92 - 97

Day 2 – **Keeping Watch**   98 - 104

Day 3 – **Signs of the Times** (Part 1)   105 - 112

Day 4 – **Signs of the Times** (Part 2)   113 - 120

Day 5 – **Staying Strong**   121 - 127

INTRODUCTION

IMAGINE FOR A MOMENT... we're seated together at a royal wedding. The invitations have been sent, all the preparations have been made, the guests have arrived, the music is playing, the flowers are spectacular ~ the sanctuary is decked for a king and queen. The bridegroom and his attendants take their places at the front.

The first strains of the wedding march begin to sound. We all rise.

It's hard to see from where we are standing off to the side. Finally, we're able to catch a glimpse of the Bride holding the arm of her father as she begins to move down the aisle toward her Bridegroom.

We crane our necks trying to take it all in. As she gets closer, we realize *something is wrong*! *It can't be – but yes*...her veil is torn, and it's askew on her head. She gets closer, and we see that is not just her veil – her hair is matted and in disarray. She looks like she just got out of bed. And her face – it's filthy; she has no makeup on.

As she walks by the row where we're standing, we get a closer look at her dress. It's unbelievable. Her gown is disheveled and wrinkled from top to bottom. It looks like it's been stuffed in a drawer for weeks. Not only that – the once-white dress is covered with an awful assortment of dark stains.

Have you ever seen such a sight? *How can this be?*

Then we see the saddest sight of all, as she approaches her Bridegroom. It's the look of profound sorrow in his eyes as he realizes that his Bride - the one he loves with all his heart – *didn't care enough to get ready for the wedding......*[ii]

The groom? Jesus Christ. The Bride? That's the *"Smokin' "HOT" Bride of Christ*. She has her dress stuffed in her dresser drawer, not realizing that any moment Jesus will return. It is time as the Bride of Christ we are **not** found *"Smokin' "HOT"* but prepared for His glorious return.

My prayer is that as your read this book the Holy Spirit will encourage you to begin preparation and propel you into a deeper and passionate love affair with Jesus. Let the primping begin!

Let us rejoice and be glad
and give him glory!
For the wedding of the Lamb has come,
*and **his bride has made herself ready**.*

Revelation 19:7 (NIV)

Chapter 1

SMOKIN' "HOT" OR "NOT"?

Yes, each of us will give a personal account to God.
Romans 14:12 (NLT)

This book was written to sound an alarm to address a crucial message that is often feared, or ignored. The day is coming when we will give a personal account to God for our lives. As His Bride, we must begin preparing ourselves NOW for eternity before it is too late! Whether we like it or not, each of us will give a personal account before Christ on how we used our gifts, talents, resources, and time for building His kingdom here on earth.

Does the thought of standing before Jesus bring a sense of confidence laced in excitement because you have been focused on eternity? Or does that thought bring feelings of fear, anxiety, or regret because you have been more focused on earthly things?

Don't zone out now and put the book down because the enemy has given you a sense of FEAR. Fear on a matter such as this, is not coming from God, but the enemy of your soul (Satan) who truly wants to see you stand before Christ smelling like smoke, naked, and ashamed. Satan wants you to have nothing to give back to the very One who sacrificed everything because of His undying love for you. Wouldn't that be tragic? Would that be devastating enough for you to allow a good healthy heart check-up from the Great Physician to be sure that you not only live a productive, joyful, and abundant life here on earth, but also hear those words we all long to hear on the Day of Judgment:

His lord said to him, 'Well done, good and faithful servant; you were faithful over a few things, I will make you ruler over many things. Enter into the joy of your lord.'

Matthew 25:21 (NKJV)

Just because we choose to ignore something, does not mean it will not happen. I was terrified of the thought of having to stand before Jesus and watch everything I ever did or said and even the motives of my heart go through the fire of His testing. It felt safer to stay in denial and hope for the best because when I thought about final testing, all I saw was lots of smoke!

I was no longer terrified when I traded in my fear for faith realizing that God will always give us everything we need to be successful and ready. The choice was mine to be prepared or not, just like it is for you.

And as we live in God, our love grows more perfect. So we will not be afraid on the day of judgment, but we can face him with confidence because we live like Jesus here in this world.

1 John 4:17 (NLT)

This Scripture gives us the "how to" or the "answer key" on what we need to do in order to stand in confidence before Christ and pass our final exam. The answer is ~ ***Grow in God's love and let that love enable you to live like Jesus here in the world!***

Living like Jesus is a process that requires Holy Spirit power to change and our willingness to learn from our mistakes. What is exciting to know is regardless of how much or little we have messed up, we can make a decision right now to live like Jesus, so we can stand confident before Him at our final exam. It is never too late as long as we are willing and still breathing.

This book was written to encourage, teach, and equip the Bride of Christ to take personal inventory of your life and make the necessary changes needed to exchange any current regrets for many future rewards.

Although we can flunk out of school by choosing not to study or get the help we need to improve our grades, we can never flunk out of God's kingdom once we have been born again and receive the Holy Spirit. According to Scripture there will be those who will receive rewards by becoming *"Rapture Ready,"* and there will be those who will suffer great loss, receive no rewards, and barely escape the wall of flames. This is the Smokin' "HOT" Bride.

But if the work is burned up, the builder will suffer great loss. ***The builder will be saved, but like someone barely escaping through a wall of flames.***

1 Corinthians 3:15 (NLT)

I have nicknamed this the "saved by the seat of your pants Christian" (if pants even would survive the heat of the fire). Notice that Scripture says that this Christian suffered GREAT loss and although they are saved, barely escaped a wall of flames which personally took on the meaning to me that they must be smelling like smoke!

As I continued to ponder this verse, I wondered what exactly a Smokin' 'Hot" Bride's life would look like. I began searching my own heart and life for similarities.

Is Paul referring to a person who is a professional church sitter who knew Scripture, who had a great deal of spiritual information, but no evidential transformation? Is it someone who believes that Christ is her Savior but outside of the church lives like the world? Or maybe this person is saved on his death bed and had no opportunity to be transformed or share the Gospel with family and friends because it was just too late. Either way, I realized that this verse was not to be ignored and had personal responsibility attached it on how it would affect our lives in eternity. This Scripture sounded an alarm deep in my spirit, compelling me to warn others that we must begin living for eternity right now.

We will discuss two Brides with two sets of consequences that are based on their free-will choice of whether to prepare for eternity or not. The *"Rapture Ready"* Bride chooses to prepare and receives rewards while the *Smokin' "Hot"* Bride declines these rewards out of fear of what it will cost her on this earth or by deliberate ignorance. Based on their choices, both Brides will bear consequences.

Over the past fifteen years of speaking and teaching engagements on the subject of transformation in various church denominations and conference settings, I have been alarmed at the lack of transformation and love we have for each other and lack of concern for and action towards the lost in our churches who profess to be Christians. They are wearing the label of saved, but their lives do not even begin to resemble Jesus.

Did you know that extensive research was conducted where 50% of people who profess to be Christians that go to church every Sunday, serve in the community, and are active in religious activities, are really **_not_** born again? These people are what I would call the "Unchurch." It is scary that they are so deceived to believe that they are destined for heaven, when Scripture indicates the contrary.

Dr. Michael J. Vlach, former Senior Writer/Researcher for Church Initiative, Inc., wrote a paper titled "Lost In Church" where he states that researcher George Barna has discovered the disturbing fact that "half of all adults who attend Protestant churches on a typical Sunday morning are not Christian." He also points out that people who call themselves Christians but are not born again are "a group that constitutes a majority of churchgoers."

Barna's findings are similar to those reported by the late Bill Bright, founder and fifty-year President of Campus Crusade for Christ. According to Bright, "Our surveys suggest that over 50% of the hundred million people in church here in the United States every Sunday are not sure of their salvation."

In addition to discovering that 50% of people in church are "lost churchgoers," the Barna Research Group has also revealed that 44% of Americans are "notional Christians." These 90 million notional Christians are people who describe themselves as Christians but do not believe that their hope for eternal life is based on a personal relationship with Jesus and the belief that He died and rose again from the dead.

According to On Mission magazine, published by the North American Mission Board of the Southern Baptist Convention, "notional Christians" do not know "whether they will experience eternal life, eternal damnation or some other outcome."

In addition to not knowing their eternal destiny, many churchgoers hold to inconsistent beliefs about how people get to heaven. In an October 2003 study, Barna revealed that 50% of professing born again Christians "contend that a person can earn salvation based upon good works." This clearly contradicts the biblical teaching that salvation is by grace alone, not by works.

The confusion of churchgoers also extends to the way of salvation. Although the Bible teaches that Jesus is the only way of salvation, Barna points out that "Many committed born again Christians believe that people have multiple options for gaining entry to Heaven."

Barna says that many who attend Protestant churches have been "anesthetized" to the Gospel. Many have mentally accepted correct beliefs but have "lived without a shred of insight into what a relationship with Christ was all about."

This shocking discovery that there are large numbers of lost churchgoers is not inconsistent with what the Bible says. In Matthew 7:21 Jesus says, "Not everyone who says to me, 'Lord, Lord,' will enter the kingdom of heaven." He also says that many will cry out, "Lord, Lord," only to hear Him say, "I never knew you" (Matt. 7:22–23). It appears that Jesus' solemn warning may apply to many who fill the church pews on Sunday mornings.[iii]

As the above research reveals, we not only have the "*Rapture Ready*" Bride, the *Smokin' "Hot"* Bride, but also the person who is not going to even appear at the Judgment Seat of Christ. The Great White Throne is reserved for unbelievers who are destined for Hell. This study not only shocked me, but was once again sounding the alarm in my spirit that it is time we wake up as His Bride and become "*Rapture Ready*".

We are not going to talk about the Great White Throne in this book because the topic of this book is to encourage the Bride of Christ to begin preparation for eternity with Jesus. My hope is that after we make the necessary adjustments to our lives through obedience and repentance, our lights will shine so brightly it will attract and invite those destined for Hell to cross over to the saving grace of Christ.

We can no longer assume that someone is the real deal just because they say they grew up in church, speak Christianese, own a Bible, and serve in the church. The Bible warns us over and over again about false prophets. We are to be professional fruit inspectors and not be deceived by those who say they are Christians, yet live like the world and have no evidence of the Holy Spirit. We cannot live a transformed life without the Holy Spirit, who gives us the power we need to be victorious.

Will the Real Christian Please Speak Up?

Patty attended church, believed she was going to heaven, and prayed religious prayers she learned in Sunday School.

Patty was forty-eight years old when she cried out to God for help and salvation after having major surgery and suffered the tragic loss of her husband to suicide. This time her prayer was different because it came from her broken heart in desperate need and not one of her usual religious prayers. She knew deep down in her spirit that something had changed and although her circumstances did not, something inside of her did.

Her close friends were not churchgoers nor were they interested in her spiritual encounter. She was determined to find God and began seeking Him in a local church, even if it meant doing it alone. She found a little church down the street where she began to attend Sunday Services along with Bible study. Patty was excited to be around a group of Christians who she believed could help her grow, answer questions, and show her how to live a successful Christian life.

As she began attending Bible study, she noticed that the church members were disgruntled at the new Pastor and that division, bitterness, and fighting were the main topics of the Bible study hour. Patty knew she did not know much about the Bible, but she did know that their behavior was wrong. She held her tongue as she patiently waited for someone to stop the nonsense. Rather than letting the disease of division, gossip, and backbiting spread, Patty, the visitor told the group of church members that their behavior was wrong and harmful.

Patty, the new believer, needed to have a good church experience where she would be surrounded by mature Christian women who would love and help her grow in her relationship with Christ. Although she has been encouraged to try another church, she is quite disappointed and believes she can do it on her own. Patty did not experience true fellowship between believers in a good Bible study, but she did hear gossip and backbiting.

That behavior from professing Christians is exactly what Satan was hoping for. He is always looking for an opportunity to isolate believers and work on our minds to steal any seed being planted from God's word, so he can kill, steal, and destroy. Jesus warns us about this in His parable of the farmer scattering the seed in the Book of Mark, Chapter 4.

The farmer plants seed by taking God's word to others. The seed that fell on the footpath represents those who hear the message, only to have Satan come at once and take it away. The seed on the rocky soil represents those who hear the message and immediately receive it with joy. But since they don't have deep roots, they don't last long. They fall away as soon as they have problems or are persecuted for believing God's word. The seed that fell among the thorns represents others who hear God's word, but all too quickly the message is crowded out by the worries of this life, the lure of wealth, and the desire for other things, so no fruit is produced.

Mark 4:14-19 (NLT)

We are to call the enemy out in the open when he is at work in our lives and those who profess they believe in Christ, so we can correct our behavior where needed, grow closer and more powerful for His glory.

It is time that we as the *"Rapture Ready"* Bride hold one another accountable in love and stop using the **"Don't Judge Me Card"**! We don't speak up and correct one another to purposely make others feel condemned, but only as a way to allow the Spirit to convict us to change our behavior, so we give God the glory with our actions and not Satan.

Bad behavior is not of God, and we must start listening to each other and paying attention to be sure that Satan is not having his way in our church and our home. It is time to make a commitment to live a life that glorifies God by obeying His word and stop compromising.

As I minister to many different age groups and denominations, there appears to be one thing in common among those confessing to being Christians, and that is a major identity crisis. How many times have you been told from people who have declined to come to church, it was because they had a bad experience with the way they were treated, felt judged, and unaccepted? Or they have friends who are Christians and think they are hypocrites because they say one thing and do another.

Don't you think it is time we wake up and start taking our Christian walk seriously? Jesus is coming back for a holy and spotless Bride, and we can either be *Smokin' "Hot"* or we can be excited for His glorious return and found prepared as we take an account for our lives here on earth. We must sound an alarm for the sleeping Bride to wake up before it is too late with hopes she will listen, take action, and one day hear from our Lord and Savior, "Well done, my good and faithful servant!"

Some will hear a "well done" at the Judgment Seat of Christ and some according to 1 Corinthians 3:15 will be getting into eternity smelling like smoke! The questions I had to ask myself was, "Who do I want to be?" Do I want to have a pitiful and nonproductive life or a powerful, purposeful, and productive life that glorifies God? Is living like the world worth taking the risk of not getting in at all? How will I feel having nothing to lay at Jesus' feet as a love offering for all that He did for me? Let's be honest, there are more people professing to be Christians today than ever before, yet so few have a testimony of transformation or look, act, and conduct themselves any different than the world.

Even though Patty was a new believer, she knew immediately in her spirit that someone needed to intervene and stop the conversation because it did not please God. I believe that the Holy Spirit sent Patty, even though she was a new believer and a visitor, to speak the truth for repentance and conviction among the believers and to expose the plans of the enemy whose purpose is always to cause division within the church.

Whether they repented and were grateful for the truth spoken, I do not know. What is important is that God's people start holding each other accountable to God's word and shine the light on Satan the minute he rears his ugly head trying to cause trouble.

The Smokin' "HOT" Church of Corinth

Let's take a look at Scripture and learn about a church that the Apostle Paul planted in Corinth where he spent three years teaching, baptizing, and leading others to Christ. Shortly after Paul returned back to his missionary journey, things began falling apart. An urgent letter was sent to Paul explaining how the believers in the church were behaving badly and returning back to their old ways of living. Paul wrote back and immediately scolded them boldly in his letter telling them it was time to grow up spiritually and stop behaving like babies. Many Christians today would have played the "don't judge me card" to protect and justify their actions. However, Paul wouldn't have bought into that excuse because he loved them too much to allow them to run back to the road of destruction. As their spiritual mentor, Paul knew it was his responsibility to confront the issue immediately in love and truth.

The Corinth church was only four years old at the time when Paul wrote 1 Corinthians. I found it quite interesting that Paul

The Smokin' "HOT" Bride of Christ

believed that after being a Christian for four years he expected them to be spiritually mature knowing these things already. Paul not only scolded them for their behavior, but also instructed them to start handling their situations among one another in a biblical manner that honored God and not in the court system. Paul understood by personal experience the power of a transformed life that these Christians were capable of having because they were believers. The city's corrupt nature also made it an excellent opportunity for the church to display to the Roman world the transforming power of Jesus Christ for others to be saved.

Let's review 1 Corinthians Chapter 3 together and why I would call the church in Corinth a church full of *Smokin' "Hot" Brides*, similar to many of our churches today because of the lack of accountability to one another.

Brothers and sisters, I could not address you as people who live by the Spirit but as people who are still worldly—mere infants in Christ. I gave you milk, not solid food, for you were not yet ready for it. Indeed, you are still not ready. You are still worldly. For since there is jealousy and quarreling among you, are you not worldly? Are you not acting like mere humans? For when one says, "I follow Paul," and another, "I follow Apollos," are you not mere human beings? What, after all, is Apollos? And what is Paul? Only servants, through whom you came to believe—as the Lord has assigned to each his task. I planted the seed, Apollos watered it, but God has been making it grow. So neither the one who plants nor the one who waters is anything, but only God, who makes things grow. The one who plants and the one who waters have one purpose, and they will each be rewarded according to their own labor. For we are co-workers in God's service; you are God's field, God's building.

1 Corinthians 3:1-9 (NIV)

There are a lot of nuggets here in these few verses. Remember Paul wrote this letter to a church full of professing Christians who accepted Christ as their Savior. Paul is shining the light directly on their issues of jealousy and fighting among one another. He also scolds them for focusing on who their human leaders are instead of keeping their eyes on Christ.

Every Christian (including leadership within churches) has an assignment to plant and water seeds. We plant and water as His gardeners by sharing the Gospel of Christ. It is ONLY through God and the work of His Holy Spirit that makes things grow. In other words, we are ALL co-workers in putting the puzzle together, and we should work together in unity fulfilling this purpose to draw others to Christ. If we are walking in unity, there is peace (God), when there is jealousy and fighting there will be division (Satan). Let's continue.

By the grace God has given me, I laid a foundation as a wise builder, and someone else is building on it. But each one should build with care. For no one can lay any foundation other than the one already laid, which is Jesus Christ. If anyone builds on this foundation using gold, silver, costly stones, wood, hay or straw, their work will be shown for what it is, because the Day will bring it to light. It will be revealed with fire, and the fire will test the quality of each person's work.

1 Corinthians 3:10-13 (NIV)

Notice that Paul uses the analogy of all Christians being builders of God's kingdom and the importance of always laying the foundation with Christ first and then everything else is to be built upon that. Paul also tells us to use extreme care and only use good materials in building. He warns not to cut corners (compromise) because the Day is coming when everything will be revealed and brought to light.

Paul says our work will be revealed with fire that will test the quality of our building materials. He is talking about when we take an account for our lives before Christ, and the choices we make while on earth.

Have you ever been involved in new construction where the builder decides to cut costs and uses cheaper materials like imitation brick panels? The imitation brick panels look like real brick, and it is not until you touch it that you realize it is a good fake. Brick is solid and considered good material that will not burn. However, imitation brick panels are much cheaper and will immediately go up in smoke. Paul is instructing us that as builders of God's kingdom here on

17

earth, we must build with the best of materials and not compromise. In other words, we should build God's kingdom with honesty, integrity, character, good motives and lots of love.

If what has been built survives, the builder will receive a reward. If it is burned up, the builder will suffer loss but yet will be saved—even though only as one escaping through the flames.

1 Corinthians 3:14-15 (NIV)

We need to take inventory of our lives and check our building materials often. Some are going to receive rewards, and some will feel relief because they made it into eternity but also regret because they have nothing that survived through the fire. You may be wondering how someone can feel relief and regret at the same time. Let's pretend your home just caught on fire, and you were able to get your spouse, children and animals to safety. You are devastated as you stand there watching everything you worked so hard for go up in smoke including keepsakes and family heirlooms. However, the moment you glance over at your loved ones and animals, you feel relieved that no one was harmed and survived. I believe that this is the best way for me to describe how we can feel both joy and regret at the Judgment Seat of Christ.

Don't you know that you yourselves are God's temple and that God's Spirit dwells in your midst? If anyone destroys God's temple, God will destroy that person; for God's temple is sacred, and you together are that temple.
Do not deceive yourselves. If any of you think you are wise by the standards of this age, you should become "fools" so that you may become wise. For the wisdom of this world is foolishness in God's sight. As it is written: "He catches the wise in their craftiness" and again, "The Lord knows that the thoughts of the wise are futile." So then, no more boasting about human leaders! All things are yours, whether Paul or Apollos or Cephas or the world or life or death or the present or the future—all are yours, and you are of Christ, and Christ is of God.

1 Corinthians 3:16-23 (NIV)

Paul expected these spiritual four-year-old Christians to know who they were and who they belonged to. He also warned them not to deceive themselves thinking they were wise by the world's standards and to stay alert to the battle between the flesh and the spirit. We must never forget that God's ways are the exact opposite of the world's ways, and we are constantly transforming until we meet Christ.

Let's review and take note of what was going on at the church in Corinth thousands of years ago is also taking place in our lives and worship services today:

- The Church was split by division of human leaders – People in the church were claiming to be followers of Apollos, Paul and Peter.

Our loyalty to human leaders must **never** divide Christians into camps or cliques. We must love and care for each other and stop fighting. Our allegiance and focus must be on Jesus and not on each other or our denominations. The Corinthian's were identifying themselves as followers of a specific Christian leader rather than followers of Christ. How many believers today claim to be a follower of a Christian leader, Pastor, or even denomination instead of a follower of Jesus Christ?

- The Church in Corinth was infected with spiritual immorality.

I found it interesting during my study that if someone was practicing sexual immorality, getting drunk, or if someone was considered evil or unworthy, they would say "they were acting like a Corinthian!" In their culture, they used the word "Corinthian." In our culture, we refer to this person as being *"lost"* or *"prodigal"*. The church of Jesus Christ must NEVER compromise with sinful ideas and practices. We should not blend in with the world culture, and we must live up to God's standards of morality by not accepting immoral behavior even if society accepts it. Just because the government makes sin legal does not mean it is right. We are to be in the world, but not of it.

We are in a constant daily battle that is no different than the Christians in Corinth, who were also struggling with their sinful environment. Surrounded by corruption and every conceivable sin, they felt the pressure to adapt. They knew they were free in Christ, but they did not understand how to live it out. The church was being undermined by immorality and spiritual immaturity. Not to mention there were also many who thought they were true believers when in fact, they were not. They had head knowledge, religion and lots of information, but no transformation.

The church is like a beautiful cruise ship on a missionary journey. We all know how amazing it is to begin a journey on a cruise ship launched out in the ocean, but we also know how tragic it is when the ocean gets into the ship. Sooner or later if the water leak is not stopped, the ship is going to sink. To avoid becoming another *"Titanic"*, it is time for us to become *"Rapture Ready,"* hold one another accountable in love and stop the massive leak because we will never know the day, or hour of His return.

1 Corinthians is one of many books that I believe needs to be read for personal spiritual inventory. The Apostle Paul confronted the Corinthians about their sins and shortcomings for no other reason but out of love. When you love someone, you tell them the truth even when it is not popular because you want them blessed and safe. We are all called to be accountable to one another and watch out for deception that will bring harm to our brothers, sisters, and the cause of Christ.

Dear brothers, if anyone has slipped away from God and no longer trusts the Lord and someone helps him understand the Truth again, that person who brings him back to God will have saved a wandering soul from death, bringing about the forgiveness of his many sins.

James 5:19-20 (TLB)

We are His Bride, His Body, and His Church that are called to work together and give Him all the glory. We are to protect and love one another by taking out the trash in our personal lives and places of worship, so God and the Holy Spirit can have center stage, and people can be saved, healed, and set free from destructive habits.

As I mentioned earlier in this book, I am going to be talking about two Brides. One who makes herself ready and other, by choice does not prepare for the big day.

The *"Rapture Ready"* Bride

The Bride that is willing to make the necessary changes to be prepared, ready and waiting for Jesus is who I will be referring to as the *"Rapture Ready"* Bride in this book. Whether this Christian will be taken up at the time of Christ's coming (Rapture) or met Him in glory (died before the Rapture), the *"Rapture Ready"* Bride lives or lived a transformed life and was found prepared and ready to receive her rewards at the Judgment Seat of Christ.

A *"Rapture Ready"* Bride understands the process of transformation and renews her mind often by studying God's word. She understands testing as a way to grow her faith and to find out if she is prepared to advance further in her call. She knows that trials will come and does her best to find the treasure in each of them to use for her benefit as she continues to build God's kingdom.

She hates it when she fails by allowing fear or her human flesh to advance but knows the power of repentance, to change her course of habit to crucify the flesh and the resurrection power within her to start over and retest as many times as it takes in order to proceed forward on her God given destiny.

The *"Rapture Ready"* Bride understands the importance of preparation and is embracing this message like never before. She welcomes Godly instruction, accountability, purification, and desires holiness in all areas of her life. The *"Rapture Ready"* Bride wants to collect as many rewards as possible, because she understands it is for her work that glorifies her Bridegroom that she can't wait to lay at His feet.

Smokin' "Hot" Bride

The *Smokin' "Hot"* Bride is also a born again believer, who has the same opportunity to fulfill her purpose and call for the cause of

Christ, but for some reason entered in by the skin of her teeth. This Bride suffers a great loss and enters into eternity empty handed.

But if the work is burned up, the builder will suffer great loss. **The builder will be saved, but like someone barely escaping through a wall of flames.**

1 Corinthians 3:15 (NLT)

This verse rocked my world where I took action and began taking my daily personal inventory on how I was living. With the Holy Spirit's help, He began shining the light of truth in areas of my life that needed immediate attention. During this process of needed revelation, I was able to confess, repent, change my direction, see prayers answered, and experience a more passionate relationship with Jesus.

Just as a student moves from grade to grade advancing forward in his education, we too can be promoted and advance to fulfill our call, as we become teachable and obedient to God's word and His Holy Spirit. Although we may have to retest over and over again in areas where we have not crucified our flesh yet, the Holy Spirit is always waiting and ready to assist. He was sent to each of us as our personal assistant to teach, guide, convict and lead us in the way that always points towards Christ. I consider the Holy Spirit the divine wedding planner as He is here to prepare us not only for the Judgment Seat of Christ but also the wedding of the universe where everyone will be watching.

As any student who wants to pass to the next grade, our responsibility is never to give up, be willing to start over as many times as it takes, stay teachable, and do what needs to be done. If we can embrace this mindset, we will be transformed from glory to glory to look like Jesus here on earth and can stand before the Judgment Seat of Christ in confidence that we will have plenty of rewards to lay at the feet of Jesus!

If you are breathing, which you are because you are reading this book, then you still have time to radically take a mess and turn it into a message that will glorify God and give you an outrageously blessed life here on earth.

God's love, grace, and mercy are new every day. That gives us the ability to start over as many times as necessary to fulfill our purpose and call on this earth that draws others to Christ.

Although Scripture is clear that our eternal destiny is not in question, the size and scope of our rewards are.

If you feel troubled and overwhelmed because you have not been living right or have some regrets, cheer up because the Holy Spirit is bringing this to your attention for your own good. You now have the opportunity by your freewill to do some housecleaning and make things right while you are still here on earth. It is never too late to start over with God. Sometimes, it takes a good nudge from the Holy Spirit and Scripture like this that deals with a serious issue that will get us moving in the right direction that will matter for eternity.

Right now we can trade in our ashes for beauty, mourning for joy and heaviness for praise that we cannot only enjoy in our lives today but also through eternity.

To all who mourn in Israel he will give: beauty for ashes; joy instead of mourning; praise instead of heaviness. For God has planted them like strong and graceful oaks for his own glory.

Isaiah 61:3 (TLB)

With knowledge, comes responsibility and now that we understand that we will all take account for our lives, it is up to us to partner with God and His Holy Spirit to begin the renovation process

If I had not come and spoken to them, they would not be guilty of sin; but now they have no excuse for their sin.

John 15:22 (NIV)

If we know what is right and choose to ignore it anyway, we are making a choice to disobey God and live in sin. That is exactly what the enemy wants. Satan wants us to have a wasteful, pitiful, and ineffective life here on earth so we are miserable, and no one will be attracted to Christ through our lives and testimony.

So any person who knows what is right to do but does not do it, to him it is sin.

James 4:17 (AMP)

There are far too many Christians who are fearful of end times and the Judgment Seat of Christ because of the lack of good biblical teaching and real understanding of the resurrection power that lives inside of every blood bought believer. Today is your D-Day, where you can decide just to hope you make it to the Judgment Seat of Christ, or use the freewill that God has given you to choose a blessed and abundant life that glorifies God where you can stand confident before Christ as a victorious overcomer.

As you discover the truth in God's word along with the resurrection power that resides inside of every born again believer, you will ignite a purposeful and passionate life for Christ that no man on earth and no devil in Hell can put out!

What if today was the day that Jesus came for His Bride, the Church? Will he find you *Smokin' "Hot"* or *"Rapture Ready"*?

Father God, I come to you in the Name of Jesus and ask that you anoint my eyes to see, my ears to hear, and my heart to receive what you would have for me in this message. I ask for wisdom and the power of the Holy Spirit to reveal, teach, and guide me as He shines a light in all areas of my life as I take a personal inventory. I want to be Rapture Ready, so Father, change, mold, and create in me a new spirit and a new heart that will glorify You. Amen!

Chapter 2

TIME TO REPAIR, RENOVATE OR REBUILD

But if we confess our sins to him, he is faithful and just to forgive us our sins and to cleanse us from all wickedness.

1 John 1:9 (NLT)

I pray that this book has encouraged and motivated you to become *"Rapture Ready"* as you prepare your mind, body and spirit for His glorious return.

I also pray that the Holy Spirit has pointed out some areas in your life that need attention, as He has done with me, so we can exchange any possible regrets for many rewards.

Just because I wrote the message does not exempt me from having to make changes in my life. I assure you that I am in the process of repairing and renovating areas of my life that the Holy Spirit has pointed out, too. I also had to face the truth that some areas of my life are beyond repair and must be completely demolished so I can start over and rebuild. It is not an easy process, but with God's help, anything is possible.

Many professing Christians cannot even begin to live a *"Rapture Ready"* life because they are holding onto the trash of their past, which is causing them to be shackled in shame, fear, guilt and bitterness.

Let me assure you that God will take our trash and turn it into triumph and our mess into a message to help others. How fast we are to throw out things that we think have no value, including our gifts and talents, because we believe a lie that was spoken over us or experienced an event we think we can't forgive or for which we can't receive forgiveness.

In the following chapters, I have included stories from my book, *Broken Hearts Have NO Color*, of those who were once *Smokin' "Hot"* but chose to become *"Rapture Ready"*. These stories are from women and one man who have different denominational preferences, backgrounds and life circumstances. The only thing they have in common is they professed to be Christian. Pay attention that some were raised in the church as Christians, others left because they were in a *Smokin' "Hot"* Church.

Satan attacked and tried to stop these *Smokin' "Hot"* Christians from reaching their divine destinies, only to be halted by their willingness to surrender, confess, repent and submit to the power of Almighty God. These *Smokin' "Hot"* Christians took their messes and turned them into messages to encourage you that regardless of your past mistakes, you can be forgiven, washed clean and become *"Rapture Ready."* Never forget that it doesn't matter how you start; it only matters how you finish.

God enjoys doing amazing things in our lives and will give us beauty for ashes if we are *willing* to give Him the ashes. Will you join me as we pile up our trash, take it to the dump, place it in the incinerator and lay the ashes at our Father's feet in exchange for beauty? I pray you will, and after you read these testimonies, make the decision to renew your commitment to Christ and live a *"Rapture Ready"* life that draws others to Him as we wait for His glorious return!

Smokin' "Hot" to "Rapture Ready"

Chapter 3

DOES ANYBODY SEE HER?

By Shannan

When you think of the world in which we live in, what comes to mind? Do you see a homeless person who is riding the city bus all day simply because it gives him a warm place to stay even if it is just for the day? Do you see the teenager walking down the side of the road in the middle of the day and wonder why they are not in school and if their parents know where he is? Do they even care? Do you notice your co-worker who just found out that her husband has been cheating on her and is now vomiting her lunch thinking if she were just a little skinnier he might love her, and she would be enough for him? Do you see the father who leaves his two young children in the back of a car left running while he slips into the local gas station only to emerge with a case of beer under his arm while cussing to his wife on the other end of the phone? Or how about the girl on your daughters cheerleading squad who just found out that she is pregnant again and thinks that one more abortion really isn't a big deal. After all, the first two helped take care of the problem her boyfriend refused to deal with, and it's not as bad as everyone says it is.

We don't have to look too far to see that pain and suffering is all around us. The ways in which many people seek to escape the pain often leave them feeling exhausted, empty and hopeless. From television, to food addictions, the internet, to "happy hour" at the corner bar, people are constantly looking for ways to quench a thirst that can truly only be met by one person. That one person is Jesus Christ.

Why then do we seek answers in everything else but Him? Often it comes from the way we were raised or experiences we had grown up with or without the church. I was raised in church and as a little girl I went to church religiously. I can honestly say that I missed only two days of church in eighteen years.

As I got older I began to dread going to church because I viewed it as more of an obligation, rather than an invitation to participate in something bigger than myself. It was more about religion than relationship, and by the time I left home for college I was bound and determined that I would spread my wings, assert my authority over myself and not go if I didn't feel like it. That also meant lying to my mom just to keep her off my case, but I knew that going through the motions was getting me nowhere and that if God wanted to meet with me, He would let me know.

When I was twenty-one years old I had decided that going to college two hundred miles away from my parents really wasn't quite far enough and that six hundred miles ought to do the trick. Coupled with naive dreams of making it big in the music industry along with an adventurous and free spirit, I ran a hundred miles an hour in the wrong direction!

Soon after arriving in Nashville, without knowing a soul, I quickly found myself attracted to the bright lights of the big city in the hope of making it big in the music industry. Along the way, I had made a few friends and after batting my eyes in several different directions was sure I had found Mr. Right. Despite the fact that I had convinced myself I would never meet a man I was going to marry in a bar, I threw caution to the wind and became heavily involved with a Disc Jockey, who worked in, of all places, a bar.

Some of my new-found friends were able to see, what unfortunately I could not, and gently tried to steer me towards a slightly less perilous lifestyle. However in my infinite wisdom I was certain that I had things under control. Never mind the fact that I was spending five nights a week in a bar, I was driving home drunk, or that I was engaging in unsafe sex with a man who struggled with commitment. What I didn't realize is that I was seeking to quench a "thirst" that only one person could fill.

I managed to find a church pew now and then partly from guilt, but mostly because I knew my mom would ask if I went to church and I hated to keep lying to her. I even had a couple of friends invite me to try their church. However, since it was an invitation to a different denomination from what I was raised in, I quickly poo-pooed the experience. Raising hands and shouting Hallelujah was a bit much for me and besides I didn't need more rules and condemnation.

Once again I reasoned that if God wanted to speak to me He would let me know. And He did!

After two years and many tears later, it had become painfully obvious that I was right. I wasn't going to find my future husband in a bar, and that included the Disc Jockey working in the bar. I had been living with him for a couple of months trying to get on my feet, and it was during this time I had come to the stark realization that he was Mr. Wrong.

I found myself lying, stealing, and constantly enduring pressure from him to use drugs. I was certain he was cheating on me, yet it took the harsh words of a woman I was working with at the time before the light finally came on.

I'll never forget that day I was boo hooing about the predicament I had found myself in and was hoping she would offer me a pat on the back and a word of encouragement telling me everything was going to be okay. Instead, she looked at me straight in the face and said "You realize that you're just prostituting yourself don't you? Can't you see he's using you?" It took the wind right out of me. I didn't want to believe her, but everything in my spirit knew she was right.

I immediately took steps to secure my own place and planned to cease all contact with him as soon as I moved out of our apartment. Unfortunately, it was a little too late. The day I signed the lease on my apartment; I totaled my truck and a week later I found out I was pregnant!

If God was trying to get my attention…He had it now. I was ready to talk and I gave Him an ear full, "God I'm sorry, please, please forgive me. Why would you let this happen to me, what did I do to deserve this? I suppose you're just punishing me and trying to teach me a lesson? God I promise I'll be good from now on. I'll do whatever you want. Please God just make this problem go away"! But in His infinite wisdom, God answered with a big resounding NO!

I knew I couldn't tell my parents I was pregnant, they would either kill me or disown me. I knew telling my boyfriend wasn't an option, he'd just ask me to get an abortion. So there I was scared and alone. The only person I could think to turn to was a friend who had invited me to church.

She supported me and prayed for me, but more importantly she invited me into the body of Christ. Immediately I was surrounded by Godly women in a mom's group that never judged me, but extended to me the grace that was present in their own lives. It was through a friend who looked past the scarlet letter and a group of women that withheld lofty glances and judgment that ultimately opened up the door for me to receive God's grace.

Ten years later and I can see the Lord's plans for me and they are full of hope. Jeremiah 29:11 (KJV) says *"For I know the thoughts that I think toward you, saith the LORD, thoughts of peace, and not of evil, to give you an expected end."*

I am grateful now that God didn't just "make my problem go away". It is because of my son that I met my husband and now also have a beautiful daughter. It is because of my son that I was able to discover a relationship with Christ beyond the confines of religion. And it is because of my son that I am believing the work of Jesus will be continued to reach his biological father.

The Bible tells us in James 1:22 (KJV): *"But be ye doers of the word, and not hearers only, deceiving your own selves".* If you are like me and have spent the majority of your life thinking that just showing up to church qualified you as having served God, then you are not alone. While just showing up to church qualified me for good attendance it made me "merely a hearer of the word" and not a doer. I was deceived to think otherwise.

1 Peter 4:9-10 (KJV) says: *"Use hospitality one to another without grudging. As every man hath received the gift, even so minister the same one to another, as good stewards of the manifold grace of God"*. I realized that God has placed in each one of us a gift for the very purpose of serving those around us and by acknowledging the gifts He has placed in us we are better prepared to be active doers of the word and to be an instrument of God's Grace. Never have I seen this demonstrated more clearly than in my own life.

When I look back on my life, I am able to see the hand of God at work. After all these years of misperception about church, I am finally able to understand that the church is not limited to the building, but goes much deeper, as the living, breathing body of Christ that can eternally affect the lives of those around us.

I want to encourage you through my personal story to begin to look at those around you in your everyday life. I challenge you to be ever mindful of the people God places in your path and to view each person as an opportunity to express the love of Christ to in a tangible way. You never know you may be able to help that girl or woman running a hundred miles an hour in the wrong direction just like me!

Chapter 4

IT'S ONLY A BOOK!

By Betty

The earliest memory I have while searching my past is hiding in the linen closet for what seemed like hours at a time because I was so afraid. I remember being awake while everyone else was asleep through the night because I was so afraid.

I also remember things that were good like my grandmother whom I loved that lived down the street from us and several good friends I had whom I played with. My father's parents lived in a rural community and were very stern and not very loving. I never enjoyed going to their house. In later years, my father told me that he never remembered my grandparents ever asking about his day, telling him they loved him, or ever giving any indication that he was loved and appreciated.

My father did not attend church, but two of his brothers became Christians and were very loving and kind. However, my memory of those gatherings was of the men gathered on the front porch, smoking, chewing and drinking.

My father became a working alcoholic and was a hard worker. When he came home is when he did his drinking and became harsh and cruel. My father never hit my mother but their arguments were loud and scary. When they argued, I hid. When I got older, I would just climb a tree and read a book.

We moved out of state when I was ten years old and that is when my addiction to reading began. We lived in a series of homes, sometimes moving three times a year, which meant three different schools. I was very shy, and it took me a while to make new friends. It seemed that every time I would make a friend, we would move again. This was a very difficult and painful time for me as a young girl and reading became my escape for many years to come.

Many years later, I met my precious husband at church but at first I didn't like him. We started dating and all we did was talk, talk, talk. Because we talked so much, he was the first person who truly knew my heart and soul. My husband was blessed to have a faithful Sunday School teacher who visited him and always showed him the love of Jesus while he was growing up. He also had a good friend who invited him to come to church. Because of the love they showed him, my husband had not only grown into a very Godly man, but he also became a preacher.

So now I am a preacher's wife. However, the addiction I had as a child for reading was still with me. I read incessantly. If I didn't have a book to read, I was frantic. I would go anywhere and do whatever it took to get a book. I didn't care what kind of book it was. I had to have a book! It was my drug of choice. It lifted me out of myself and transported me to a different plane. I neglected many things because I was reading. I read while cooking (burned quite a few meals), washing dishes, sweeping floors, you name it. I constantly had to have a book in my hand. It was so consuming that many nights I would read the entire night, and struggle to do what needed to be done the next day. I was totally out of control.

finally came to myself and realized what a hold, an addiction I had to reading when we had gone to my husband's father's funeral. There was a huge snowstorm which covered the entire east coast and we couldn't get back home. We were stuck at our son's house for almost a week and I ran out of books! Horrors! I remembered seeing a used book store several blocks away. I got to the store and although I realized it was a pornography shop, I went in anyway and bought a used Harlequin Romance novel. You could just imagine the stares that I received from the men in the store. One of the men said, *"I never saw anything like this before."* After satisfying my addiction and where it took me to have a book in my hand, I was so ashamed that I prayed to God to deliver me from that problem. God heard my broken and contrite heart to free me and He did!

I still like to read, but I no longer HAVE to read. I no longer MUST read the entire book before I put it down. And I ONLY read Christian books. God gave me a miracle that day that I will cherish forever.

People chuckle with respect when I tell them I understand their addictions because of my past addiction to reading books. They think that reading cannot be as harmful as other addictions. I believe that any addiction, anything that we put above God (work, drugs, alcohol, reading, etc.) is a sin when you are consumed by it and it rules you. The question should always be what is the root of that addiction? What caused me to be so consumed with reading that I always wanted to escape from reality? Isn't that where addictions usually start?

God gave me another miracle thirty-five years ago. My husband was the Pastor of his first church and while there, I became seriously ill with gall bladder disease. The doctors couldn't figure out what was wrong. Test after test was run, but no one could figure out what the problem was. I was told it was all in my mind. I finally had an exploratory surgery where they discovered my gall bladder was so diseased that it couldn't absorb the dye used in the tests. The doctor told me I was a hairs breath from dying.

I was in the hospital a week with a roommate I couldn't stand. She was everything I was not. She was a barmaid, she drank, she cussed and I didn't like her. I didn't like her at all! We were both scheduled to be dismissed the same day. As we were lying in our beds in complete silence waiting for the doctor to come dismiss us, a voice came very strongly in my mind saying, *"Tell her I love her"*. The great Christian that I was, I said, *"NO, I don't like her!"* The voice came again saying, *"You must tell her I love her."* With a heart full of bitterness I said, *"Do you know God loves you?"* then turned towards her with a frown on my face to see her reaction.

She looked at me with pain and unbelief on her face and replied, *"No, I didn't!"* My heart broke! I saw that the great sinner in that room was NOT her, but ME! I knew better. She didn't. Praise God, she accepted the gift God offered.

I truly believe that my hospital visit was not about my sickness but about her salvation and about the condition of my heart. A lot of the feelings I had towards my roommate in the hospital resulted from the anger I had bottled up towards alcohol and how it affected my father and our relationship. I wanted nothing to do with *anything* alcoholic.

However, at that very moment God worked a miracle in my life of beginning to have a great love for those who are trapped in addictions. Yes, that experience birthed the beginning of a ministry dear to my heart that enables me to do the work I now do, founding and administrating a rehabilitation halfway house for those ladies who come out of jail and want to get help. God has certainly had His hand on my heart and on this ministry. All the praise is due to Him!

I love God with all my heart and mind. I could not do the work He has given me without constant prayer, constantly being covered with the armor of God and daily asking for strength and wisdom. I am so grateful that He allows me to grow day by day. I know the day I stop growing will be the day I graduate from this life into His Heavenly home. I am so glad that He gives us chance after chance to grow and become more like Jesus. He never gives up on us!

Through it all, God who began a good work in us, IS going to bring it to completion if we just step out of the way and allow God to be God and allow the work to be done in our hearts. My part is to be continuously willing to grow, change and be transformed.

Chapter 5

LIFE BEYOND REGRET

By Jami

Falling leaves and fall festivals are sure signs that autumn has arrived. Every year our church hosts a Fall Festival, and every year we anticipate this fun-filled event. This year, to our delight, we had a new attraction, the monstrous slide, brother to the famous moonwalk.

Children climbed furiously to reach the pinnacle so they could feel the wind in their hair and butterflies in their stomachs as they plummeted to the bottom. My four-year-old son, James, was no exception. He could not take his eyes off that slide.

"That one, I want to go on that one," he insisted. So he went. His older sister, Madelyn, carefully helped him up the swaying path to the top, but just as they reached the platform from which they would slide, James obviously looked down, realized how high off the ground he was, and quit moving forward. His little body began tugging against Madelyn's helping hands. I could see the agitation in her face and the fear in his, but there was no turning back. The only way down was to slide.

Oh, how I wanted to rescue my all-too-eager son, but I felt helpless. Gently, but firmly, Madelyn grabbed him, and they began the two-second free fall down the breath-taking slide. It was over almost before it began, but James was not happy!

The next morning as we discussed the previous night's events and attractions, James told me that the Fishing Booth was his favorite. Madelyn said she liked the slide. "Did the slide scare you a little, James?" I asked. "No," he replied. I was surprised by his response, so I didn't say anything. A few moments later James announced, "It didn't scare me a little bit; it scared me a lot!"

I laughed to myself as I thought about the honesty in my son's reply. As I thought about his scary little experience, I was reminded of a time in my life when I felt trapped and scared—not just scared a little bit, but scared a lot!

Lured by the promise of love and acceptance, the "fall festival slide" in my life was pre-marital sex. I insisted on taking a chance and quickly found myself at the top of a very tall slide looking down—terrified of what I saw. I wasn't looking down at the ground; I was staring down at two blue lines. The pregnancy test was positive. Paralyzed by fear, I saw the harsh reality of pre-marital sex. The "slide" didn't seem so attractive and alluring now. I wasn't just scared; I was petrified!

Like many others who have walked in my shoes, I didn't welcome the idea of aborting my child. However, the idea of pregnancy scared me, and abortion presented itself as the only option. Panic superseded rationale. I remember making the call to an abortion clinic as if it were yesterday. With my stomach in knots, I scheduled the appointment. Then, I waited and waited, and waited.

Those weeks were agonizing. I knew I was violating my moral code, yet, the fear of exposure, the fear of someone finding out that I had gotten pregnant, drove me to abort. I was focused on my immediate needs and did not consider the future. Emotions of that sort are difficult to explain and even more difficult to feel.

My view of abortion had always been conservative—abortion is wrong; it is murder. All that changed, however, when I faced an unplanned and unwanted pregnancy all my own. Then, thoughts such as, This will be an easy way out ... a way to not have to deal with my problem ... no one will ever know, replaced my conservative view of abortion. It's scary how personal experience can either strengthen or weaken character, values, and morals! For me, it was obviously the latter. Everything I thought to be true about myself came crumbling down all around me.

I must have lived those weeks surrounding my crisis vicariously, because looking back I remember nothing of making a sound, informed decision. There was no information; no alternative. Yet, conversely there was no voice of objection—no voice crying out for the innocent life of my child, save the brave protestors at the clinic ... but by that time, it was too late.

Cowardly, I entered the front door of an abortion clinic to end the life of my child, and after the procedure was quickly ushered out the back door. I was sent on my way with no understanding of what had occurred to my body, heart, soul, and spirit during those brief moments I lay on the sterile table of an abortionist. I bought the propaganda—abortion is the easy way out—hook, line, and sinker.

I chose to cope by separating myself from my abortion and numbing myself to the world around me. But the easy way out wasn't so easy anymore. Guilt and shame engulfed me, and like an open sore, pain oozed from my soul. I longed for forgiveness and a chance to go back and undo what had been done. The old saying that two wrongs don't make a right is so, so true. How could I have been so foolish?

Fear over the emotions I was experiencing, or better yet, trying not to experience, led to further separation and denial. I struggled to carry on with life and leave the past in the past. A part of me stuffed the pain deep down inside. I don't think I consciously chose to forget it, but subconsciously I removed myself as an active player in the decision I had made to abort. I told myself that I didn't do it. I convinced myself that it had not been me who had entered that abortion clinic ... It couldn't have been me ... I would never have done something like that. My pursuit to avoid the truth at all costs devoured my conscience.

Life after my abortion didn't change much from the life I had lived prior, yet somehow, I had developed a dead feeling about my life. I was a white-washed tomb, a newly painted house whose structure was rotting away. From all outward appearances, I was okay, but on the inside, the truth was screaming to be told ... to be heard.

"Help me! My heart cried out. "Oh, please love me ... I know I'm not easy to love ... I don't deserve love ... but please, someone please" I needed to be forgiven. I needed my innocence restored. I needed to know Jesus. But instead of embracing Him, I permitted a roller coaster ride of emotions to lead me further and further away from the One true source of love. Before long I was back at square one—pregnant again.

Could this be my second chance? Those were not the words that immediately entered my mind as the test revealed I was going to have a baby, but they were the thoughts of my heart as news of this pregnancy began to take root. This baby would be my redemption ... my atonement child.

Scared half to death, I shared the news with the baby's father, who had recently moved clear across the country to embark on a new life. He wasn't excited, but neither was he breathing down my throat to have an abortion. Relief! Although, he was not physically present with me, his calmness about our situation set me at ease.

"We'll get through this," was his answer. We talked of marriage. I begged him to marry me, and I think he wanted to, but he was scared. He wanted to do what was right, but now he was the one on top of that "slide" looking down—terrified of what he was seeing.

Days turned into weeks and weeks turned into months. I only saw him two or three times during my pregnancy, but when the time came for the baby to be born, he returned. He was a proud papa the night our daughter, Madelyn, was born. Love beamed from his eyes as he looked down at the bundle of joy he was holding in his arms. God's gift of life was ours, and we were proud parents ... but shortly after her birth, he left.

My sheer delight over Madelyn's birth was overshadowed by brief moments of torment from my past. I couldn't escape my past. I couldn't escape the fact that I was alone. Everywhere I turned, no matter how far or how hard I ran, it was always there: abortion ... loneliness ... alcohol ... neglect. The vicious cycle was once again spinning.

During my pregnancy the God of my childhood had been calling to my heart, "Come back to Me, Jami, I love you!" Oh, how I wanted what God had for me, but I was scared! I knew I would have to give up everything to follow Him. My grip was tight, and I couldn't let go of the sin that held me prisoner.

How can God forgive me? I wondered. How can I forgive myself? What in the world am I doing to this sweet and precious child of mine? Will my life ever be "normal?" Is this how I am going to live for the rest of my life? Oh, God forgive me!

Several years of living it out at the bottom of the barrel was enough for me. I was tired of running, tired of hiding, tired of doing it my way. It was the darkest time of my life, and looking back, the only way I can explain how my life changed is G-R-A-C-E! God used an extraordinary set of circumstances to call me back to Himself.

In January of 1999, I gave my life over to the Lord. I climbed into my Savior's lap and braced myself for a free fall down the "slide." For indeed, those first few years felt much like a free fall. I had been married for two months to a man I barely knew (who was not a believer), and I was again pregnant and still very insecure because of my past. But isn't God good? He blessed my feeble offering. My faith was small (I'm sure it was smaller than a mustard seed), but my God was gracious. In the spring of that same year, my husband, Brad, received Jesus as his Savior and became the leader, protector, and provider of our little family.

Easy? Not a chance. I fought Brad's attempt to lead every step of the way. Although my heart had softened to Christ, it was still rock hard to those closest to me. Brad didn't know much about my past, and I wasn't offering up any details. Our relationship before marriage had not been characterized by purity, and he knew that I had not been innocent by any means. He just didn't know how guilty I was!

My walk with the Lord did not silence my past. It was still there haunting and taunting me. But God allowed people into my life that would help pull me from my self-protective shell. He put me on the path to freedom, although it seemed that for every one step forward, I took two steps backward. At times, I thought the pain of the past would ruin my marriage and leave me crippled for life, but God continued to whisper words of hope in my ear.

Finally, the time came for me to tell Brad the truth about my past. He needed to know, but I was so scared to tell him. I feared I would see his disgust as my secret was revealed, but as I told him, I only saw love. He didn't say much, and I knew he was hurt—hurt deeply ... but he still loved me. What a beautiful picture of the love of Christ?

Working through denial, anger, and bitterness, and then extending forgiveness to myself and accepting the choice, I made to abort brought wholeness to my broken heart. Freedom didn't come over night, nor did it come easily, but if you ask me if it was worth it, I'll tell you, "Absolutely!"

God has radically changed my life, my heart, and my vision. I am no longer a tattered woman searching for love and trying to make up for the past. I am a much-loved daughter of the King ... restored and redeemed. I am a virgin bride clothed in robes of righteousness.

What happened to change my vision? God opened my eyes to the sin in my heart. He sounded the call to repentance, and I humbly responded. God made me new. He redeemed and restored me. II Corinthians 5:17 (NIV) states, *"Therefore, if anyone is in Christ, he is a new creation; the old has gone, the new has come."* God gave me a new vision of who I am in Him.

I recognized what Christ had done for me. Jesus paid the price for my sin. Oh, what an amazing and marvelous thing! While I was still a sinner, Christ died for me. (Romans 5:8) Isaiah 43:18-19 (NIV) declares, *"Forget the former things; do not dwell on the past. See, I am doing a new thing! Now it springs up; do you not perceive it? I am making a way in the desert and streams in the wasteland."* Without a doubt, God took the wastelands of my heart and made them into babbling brooks.

I realized who I was in Christ. I quit conforming to the world's view of who I was. Transformed by God's Word, I found renewal. (Romans 12:2) God's perspective of who I was in Christ transcended my thoughts and feelings of who I was. I am a treasure in the Father's hand.

I revere who I am becoming in Christ. I am striving to live in purity before my Father. Ephesians 1:4 (NIV) says, *"For he (God) chose us in him (Jesus) before the creation of the world to be holy and blameless in his sight."* Confident of His work in my life, I press forward to attain the goal to win the prize for which God has called me. (Philippians 3:14) God is still hard at work in my life, and just as He promises in His Word, His work will be continuous until the return of Jesus. (Philippians 1:6)

The enemy wants me to run from my Redeemer, and for years, I did. The bonds of sin were thick around my soul. But Christ broke the bonds. He set this captive free!

Over the years, I have learned much … lived much … fallen much … failed much, but most importantly, over the years, I have been loved much. (Romans 8:38)

Today, as God has brought beauty from ashes in my life and Brad's, we are happily married (much like newly-weds) with eight beautiful children. Madelyn, my first born, has an incredible relationship with her dad (whom our family prays for on a daily basis to come to the saving knowledge of Jesus Christ), and my oldest son, Micah, is in heaven, where I will one day hold him and tell him just how much I love him.

Jami is the founder of Abounding Grace Outreach Ministries. Jami's desire through this ministry is to encourage others to find healing and freedom in Christ.

Chapter 6

THE MODERN DAY WOMAN AT THE WELL

By Dawn

"'If abortion had been legal, you'd have never been born!" And how about living ten miles from your own daughter but never calling or asking to see her? Do you think those things might have an impact on a young person's self-worth? I can tell you from experience, those words and actions hurt. The old cliché, "sticks and stones may break my bones but words will never hurt me," does NOT hold true when it involves loved ones speaking to one another, especially if the one speaking is a parent talking to a child. That is where my story begins.

Did my mom love me when she spoke those harsh words to me? Does she love me now? I can emphatically say, "Yes, my mom loves me." Can I also say that when she was young she was angry and full of her own hurt? Yes, I can say that, too! Was my mom showing extremely bad judgment when she opened her mouth and spoke such words to me? Yes, I can say she was.

What about my biological father? Did he love me? I reckon in his own way he did. I guess he figured if I needed him, I would call. Little did he know that by not showing any interest—by not wanting to see me or spend time with me—it caused me to wonder for years why I wasn't good enough.

I am a modern day Samaritan woman—a woman very similar to the one written about in the Bible in John, chapter four. The story begins with a woman who goes all alone in the early afternoon to fetch water from a well. Jesus, who is at that well with no jar or bucket, asks her for a drink of water. During their conversation, Jesus tells her to go get her husband and come back. This is where she and I come together. The woman told Jesus she did not have a husband, and He answered, "You are right. You have had five husbands and are now living with another man." You got it! She'd had five husbands! And she was at the well to draw water when no one else was around because she was an outcast. Having multiple husbands at that point in history was **not** socially acceptable.

Now her story and my story don't exactly line up, but I have been married four times. I have two children, each with a different last name, and neither of their last names matches my current last name. So before I continue with my story, let me ask you this question: Is it socially acceptable today for a woman to have multiple marriages and children by different husbands? No, it is not.

Many times I have wanted to bow my head in shame when someone asked me where my daughter's or son's dad lived or had to explain my children's age difference and how long my current husband and I have been married.

My mistakes and bad judgment were weighing me down. How can you make new friends and invite them into your life when you believe everyone is looking at you with judging eyes?

The natural question for you to ask is, *"Were you saved when all of this was going on?"* I mean, surely a woman covered by the blood of Jesus wouldn't be married that many times or carry that much guilt. Fortunately, even though my mom and my step-dad never went to church or took my little brother and me to church, they didn't keep me from getting onto the Baptist bus that came by on Sunday mornings.

As a twelve year old, I walked, all alone, down that l-o-o-o-o-o-ng church aisle and answered the call of the Holy Spirit. I really didn't know what I was doing, and when that nice man—probably a deacon—asked me if I was a Christian, I said, "No, I'm a Methodist!" Thankfully, he rephrased the question and asked if I had Jesus in my heart? I said "YES" and was baptized a few weeks later. Even though I didn't really know what it meant to be a Christian, I was attuned to the prompting of the Holy Spirit.

I would love to report that my steps of faith at that church took me safely through adolescence, but it didn't. The hole in my heart needed human affection and affirmation. The absence of felt love left a deep emptiness that my brief relationship with God did not sustain. It was hard to appropriate the love of the Father with no spiritual encouragement at home. Although Mom supported me in other areas of my life, there was no affection and no positive response to my accomplishments. She guided us by negatives and criticism. This was the enemy's opportunity to convince me of my worthlessness and failure. Looking back through adult eyes I can see that my family members really did care deeply about me. They demanded obedience to rules as expression of their love --- yet my heart was desperate for validation as a person.

I did have the advantage of being smart, tall, pretty and athletic. That was plenty enough to keep boys in my life full time. With my longing for love and affection, sex was only a small step away. It felt good. It was a way to be "close," momentarily filling that life-long need inside me for intimacy. I was quick to say "I love you" then off to the next partner with another "I love you." I didn't think about the baggage I was piling on myself that would eventually weigh me down to destructive levels.

I seldom made it to church and didn't really derive much immediate encouragement there. Yet God used that time to remind me that He was there and He loved me. Even though that truth slipped in and out of my mind, it would prove a firm foundation down the road.

Following college I moved to a small town with a new job. Part of my new start was to begin attending church again. But a failure to solidly connect with my new church family and my lack of biblical knowledge soon discouraged me. I wasn't discouraged with meeting new guys, and unfortunately, began racking up more sexual partners. One of these men was especially nice and soon my friends were urging me to consider marriage. Even though we announced love for one another, our differences were enormous. While I agreed to a wedding, my heart told me this was a mistake. Twelve months and one affair later we divorced. Guilt and shame once again filled my broken heart.

Then along came husband number two. He was Sauvé and debonair—quite the womanizer, actually—and I fell for it hook, line, and sinker. He told me why he and his first wife had gotten a divorce and also told me about his indiscretion ... but I didn't tell him about mine. I thought, "Wow, if he had an affair, then that is what I deserve. We have a lot in common." So, we got married.

My new husband had two precious children from his previous marriage who were five and eight years old, and we had a daughter of our own (my pride and joy).

I had been attending church all this time. Now my new husband came with me and we both became very involved: Sunday school, mission trips, choir and discipleship classes. I was growing and learning but I was still so needy and was difficult to live with.

My husband eventually found his secretary to be more appealing than I was and had no problem parading her around. When I finally had enough, we divorced. But I couldn't make a clean break that time because we had a daughter. That didn't stop me, however, from quickly swinging into another unhealthy relationship.

Eventually the company I worked for relocated me to another state. The heartbreak here was that my daughter's joint custody arrangement kept her away from me for lengthy periods of time. But my solid trust in God's power carried me through.

In my new location I found a good church immediately. God put three mentors into my life who encouraged serious spiritual growth in so many areas of daily living --- but it failed to reach all of my fleshly personal habits. I spent hours walking and running while praying for God's forgiveness and total cleaning of my life. I was still hurting, but for the first time I felt free and clean. This took me closer to my Father than I had ever experienced. In spite of vowing to become sexually pure another poor decision and more trouble was close by.

With my daughter far away and time on my hands, my godly friends were not able to protect me from my "old self" indiscretions. Almost seamlessly I had returned to the bar/party scene, where I met the next significant man in my life. He was okay at first and when my daughter was around he was attentive to her. Of course he wanted to have sex --- and so we did. When at church I was that other person, wanting to live right. I would go home and tell my boyfriend that sex outside of marriage was out. His disapproval of my church life was understandable. So I quit hanging out with my Christian friends and began spending full time with his friends.

All this time the Holy Spirit was screaming to me, "Get away from him; do not marry him. LISTEN TO ME!." But I didn't listen. I heard but I didn't listen. I was like Paul in Romans 7:15: *"I do not understand what I do. For what I want to do I do not do, but what I hate, I do."* So I married again.

Our marriage was miserable. I found myself with the same old degrading, belittling behavior directed toward me. We had a big house but no friends. We hung out with his parents, who lived next door. I got pregnant immediately, and I gave birth to a wonderful little boy. At that time I gained full custody of my daughter, so now we were a family of four.

In spite of family church attendance, I soon realized this husband was not meeting my needs --- needs that only God could fill. A new friend came into the picture and he was a fresh face amidst the boredom of an unfulfilled marriage relationship. Trouble came head-on. I filed for divorce (I knew exactly how to do this by now). Because of my emotional and physical connection with my new relationship I lost custody of my son. I was shattered and broken. Added to that defeat, my pastor asked me to step away from the various church activities in which I had taken leadership. In my abandoned state I felt miles away from God.

I needed a friend, and to my surprise that friend was my mom! She moved close to me to be of help. A huge healing time began to take place inside of me and it began with the relationship between me and my mom. I was also struggling through another failed marriage. It was time to take stock and decide who I really wanted to be. That man to whom I turned in my need of true relationship became my fourth husband. Although we had been living in sin, God was at work in both of us. He, a pastor's son and me, a broken, wounded sinner, together were redeemed in a final, resolute manner.

Shortly after our marriage we answered the Holy Spirit's call and walked down the aisle together --- this time to state publicly our commitment to trust and obey our Lord as a family. Since that time, my two children have answered the Savior's call and been baptized. About that time my pastor asked me to share the story of my life. I bared my soul, and using the woman at the well in John 4 as an illustration, I revealed my past brokenness and my present victories.

God's word is true. Romans 8:1-2 says, *"...there is now no condemnation for those who are in Christ Jesus, because through Christ Jesus the law of the Spirit of life sets me free from the law of sin and death."* I am redeemed, and the enemy has no power over me! I am free from the baggage that the enemy wants me to carry! I have laid it at the cross, and today and every day I cast my burdens upon the Lord and He sustains me. (Psalm 55:22)

Like the Samaritan woman at the well, I have left my jar (my burden) at the well and am telling everyone what my Lord has done for me ... for He knows everything I have ever done and will ever do, and He still loves me and forgives me. Praise God!

"Then leaving her water jar, the woman went back to the town and said to the people, 'Come see a man who told me everything I ever did'".

John 4:28-29 NIV

Chapter 7

THE GOD WHO LAUGHED AT MY JOKES

By Laurette

When I was a little girl growing up in the suburbs of Long Island, I felt very close to God—and it wasn't the God I experienced in the church we attended. That God seemed rather distant and stuffy.

My mother enjoyed telling the story of what happened the first time we went to an Episcopal Church when I was three years old. As we sat in the crowded sanctuary that hot and humid Sunday morning I screamed, "Get me out of here!"

In time, I became accustomed to the church. I memorized the prayers and knew exactly when we were supposed to kneel, cross ourselves and answer in unison. I could mimic Father Palmer's British accent when he said that Jesus is "our only mediator and advocate." I didn't know what it meant, but I liked the way he said it. I did my best to imitate his round vowels under my breath, until my mother would tell me to stop.

How different that was from my experiences with God in my room. I had an illustrated children's Bible and enjoyed telling my stuffed animals the stories by looking at the pictures before I could read the words. I would place them in a semi-circle around me, show them the pictures, and act out the stories using a variety of different accents and animal sounds. I enjoyed seeing how many voices and characters I could create. This ability with dialects came in handy later in years as an actor, storyteller and comedienne Off-Broadway known as "The Woman of 101 Voices."

I did my best to come up with a punch line at the end of each Bible story to make God laugh. I figured He had such a hard job that He needed a good chuckle now and then.

"So God said to Noah," I told my captive audience. "'Noah, build Me an ark!' And Noah said, 'Okay, God. That's right up my alley!'" As an aside, I added, "Won't God get a kick out of that?" And I believed He absolutely did!

During the account of Daniel in the lions' den when God spared Daniel's life by closing the lions' mouths, I suggested the head lion mumbled, "No lunch today, boys." When David hurled the stone at the giant Goliath's head, it landed "smack-dab in the middle of his forehead—and you know that hurt like the Dickens," I added.

Hearing God's Voice in My Closet

As a small child, whenever someone hurt my feelings I ran home crying and hid in my bedroom closet. If Robbie said I was fat, or Willie pushed me in my little red bathing suit into the bramble bushes, or Karen didn't want to play with me, it was hard to hold back the tears. I'd run home as fast as I could. The moment the closet door was shut, I was safe. Sitting on a pile of shoes and toys, hidden among the shirts and dresses, no one could hurt me.

For three years God met me in that closet. Tears streaming down my face, I shut the door and sat in the comforting darkness. After a few moments I saw a flash of light. A bright scene appeared on the inside of the closet door as if it were a movie screen. In this open-eyed vision I stood behind a curtain and watched an adult version of myself onstage in front of a vast outdoor audience. The grown-up Laurette had one hand lifted high above her head and appeared to be speaking or singing into a microphone in the other hand. In front of me were thousands of people who also had their hands lifted toward the sky.

I instinctively knew the people were worshiping God, even

though I'd never witnessed such behavior at St. Thomas Episcopal Church. The only time I'd seen people's hands go above waist-level was to hold a hymnal. Years later I learned that was a common way to worship God in ancient Israel and the early Christian church.

After a few seconds the vision faded and I heard a comforting voice over my right shoulder. "Everything is going to be all right," He said. In my heart, I knew this was God's voice. His voice hugged me and gave me peace. "Everything's gonna be all right," I repeated after Him, sniffling and wiping my tears on my sleeve. Standing up, I opened the door and stepped out of the closet to face the world again.

This happened many times over a three-year period between the ages of three and six. Nothing seemed unusual about these encounters, probably because I had nothing with which to compare them. Whenever I was upset, I knew I could run into my closet and hide from the world, but not from God. He met me there and comforted me. He always understood, showed me what I believed was a vision of my future, and assured me everything was going to be all right. I could trust Him. He would never hurt or disappoint me.

The Wall Around Me

When I was six years old, something changed. I no longer felt that closeness with the Lord. The only way I could describe it was to say it felt like there was a thick wall around me, separating me, protecting me from everyone and everything. I felt safe inside this walled fortress, but I also felt empty and alone—except when Mommy and I would play.

We'd giggle like girlfriends as we took long walks through the neighborhood holding hands. Acting out all the characters to the *Peter Pan* album I got for Christmas, we'd fly around the playroom singing "I won't grow up!" Snuggling together on the couch we read *Little Women* aloud with English accents...

My beautiful mother Jacqueline was a petite, blue-eyed strawberry-blonde. She was brilliant and funny with a voice like warm honey; an Irish colleen who spoke fluent Spanish and enjoyed parsing words back to their Latin origins. A frustrated actor and singer, she was an attorney and the first woman Assistant District Attorney on Long Island. She later became one of only two female Assistant District Attorneys out of over 130 A.D.A.s in District Attorney Frank Hogan's office in New York City. I was so proud of her.

Although I could never believe it, I loved when people said, "You're just like your mother." She was stunning. I felt ugly. Sadly, this remarkable woman with the movie star good looks, brilliant mind and tender heart became an alcoholic who had three nervous breakdowns and attempted suicide when I was a child.

Things looked so perfect on the outside of our beautiful home on Long Island, but behind closed doors were pain, torment and tears.

To comfort myself, I developed an unhealthy attachment to food. I remember running into my parents' bedroom and kneeling beside the bed. On a bright, beautiful mid-afternoon in suburban Long Island, Mommy was asleep in her darkened bedroom. Was she depressed, or had she been drinking?

I was small, a little pudgy, with dimpled hands and knees, my round "Campbell kids" face framed with a brunette pixie cut. Tears pooled in bright amber eyes and flowed down chubby little cheeks as I patted Mommy's face.

"Mommy! Mommy!" I cried. "I can't stop eating."

For the past hour the little girl her mother called "Little Laurie So-Sweet" had been eating bread and butter, Easy-Bake Oven cake mix, cereal and anything else I could find to comfort me while Mommy slept. I was six years old and food was my friend.

At Northside Elementary School when the boys discovered I'd cry when they called me "Fatso," it became a favorite taunt. I remember many days running home from school in tears. An only child, I was unaccustomed to the teasing children often do. I didn't understand why they were so mean to me.

"I know what they're really saying," I'd tell my mother. "They're saying I have a 'fat soul,' huh Mommy?" It was a silly thing to say. I knew it wasn't true. I was just trying to ease the tension for both of us.

Once alone in my room I'd look in the mirror and scold myself, "You're fat! You're ugly! You're stupid! I hate you!" Then came the tears. After the tears came the search for food. I'd watch television and eat until I was numb. It was an unending cycle that continued for over thirty years.

I attempted my first diet when I was eleven years old. I saved up the money from my lemonade stand and secretly went into the neighborhood drug store to buy a box of *amazing* weight loss candies.

"These are for your mother, right?" the pharmacist asked, peering over his spectacles.

"Uh, yes," I lied.

One weight-loss candy was to be eaten with a glass of water in place of a meal or for a snack. I ate half the box at one sitting and hid the rest under my dresser. They were delicious. I gained three pounds.

It's surprising that I didn't become heavier than I did. I attribute this to my mother becoming the town's first "health-food nut," as people interested in nutrition were called in the 1960s. When Mom was following a healthy diet, taking vitamins and exercising daily she didn't drink alcohol as much—sometimes not at all which was marvelous to me.

While other children's lunchboxes had Twinkies and Yodels with their bologna sandwiches on white bread, I had celery sticks and apple slices with my tuna sandwich on whole grain bread. I didn't seem to mind the kids' taunts about the weird food. I made it a game. I could eat carrot sticks like a rabbit and do an impression of Bugs

Bunny to make them laugh. Ah—an audience! I loved it.

Over the next twenty-plus years, food was my primary "drug of choice." If I ate enough of it, it numbed me. Food, and later alcohol, cigarettes, drugs, reckless relationships and New Age spiritual practices were some of the things I used to fill the missing piece on the inside of me since "the wall" went up—the wall which separated me from God.

Numbness, I discovered, is a poor substitute for peace.

The Little Yogini

When I was seven years old my mother became involved in yoga. A nice-looking Asian couple had a popular daytime yoga program on television. It was scheduled right after Jack LaLanne's exercise show. It seemed so harmless, so relaxing and so *spiritual*.

The exercises relaxed Mom. Being an only child, my mother and I did almost everything together. We did yoga exercises together too. When she began teaching free yoga classes to high school and college students in our home, I was the little demonstration model. I loved the attention. My father thought it was all rather kooky, but he was busy building his law practice and didn't pay much attention to what we did when he wasn't home.

For several years Mom and I visited Ananda Ashram, a yoga retreat in upstate New York associated with Swami Satchidananda. When I was ten years old, the Swami visited the ashram while we were there and 'blessed' me. His smell was overpoweringly sweet. His long, wavy black hair was heavy with oil, and always looked wet as it flowed over his saffron shoulders. I suppose the attention was to make me feel "special." I just felt uncomfortable.

During meditation times, I wouldn't keep my eyes closed. I kept peeking at all the serene-looking adults in the room as we sat cross-legged in the lotus posture, incense filling the air. I liked doing the exercises better.

For twenty-two years I was an avid student of Hatha Yoga, and was an instructor for part of that time. I also practiced Kundalini yoga. During my late teens and twenties, I studied a variety of spiritual practices, seeking to recover the God of my childhood, although I didn't realize it at the time. I knew something was missing. Everything I studied, every conference I attended, each book I read and course I took was an attempt to find the Lord who loved me and laughed at my jokes.

My studies included a variety of metaphysical philosophies and practices from A to Z: Astrology to Zoroastrianism; Kabbalah, Mystical Christianity, Hinduism, various types of yoga; shamanism, Tibetan Buddhism, Universal Mind, Hawaiian Huna; Urantia, Course in Miracles and writings from other channeled entities, spirit guides and Ascended Masters.

"I Feel Dead Inside"

In my twenties I lived in New York City and was the typical 'struggling actor.' I lived in the East Village and worked part-time as a secretary and waitress "to support my acting habit," as I put it. I fearfully went to auditions on my days off, but most of the time I drank white wine, watched television and read New Age books.

In March 1982 I visited my mother who was working as an attorney for the Thruway Authority in upstate New York. She and my stepfather Fred were separated and Mom was very depressed. We got drunk together. "I feel dead inside," Mom said. I tried to encourage her with Tarot card readings and prompted her to get in touch with the light within, but nothing seemed to help. She said she felt as if she had no hope. There was a great sadness in her eyes. She looked lost.

A week later I got a call from Fred. My mother had aimed a .357 Magnum at her heart and pulled the trigger. She missed the first time, but the second attempt hit its mark. The first bullet lodged itself in the bedroom wall, prompting police investigators to consider her death was a homicide, but they later ruled it a suicide. I was grateful for that. As horribly painful as her death was, I couldn't stand the thought of someone else taking her life.

My boyfriend Damien and my stepfather tried to keep me out of the bedroom where Mom took her life. While they were out, I carefully wiped up her blood from the wooden floorboards and wall. I didn't want anyone else to do it. Crying, I held her hairbrush close to my face, closed my eyes and took a deep breath. Her scent was still there, but she was gone.

"You're just like your mother."

As the months passed, I drank more and went to fewer auditions. They scared me. Almost everything scared me or made me feel insecure. I walked along the streets with my eyes downcast. Talking to people frightened me, but it was easier after a few drinks.

Every so often I would hear a voice in my head say words that used to delight me, "You're just like your mother." Who said that? Where did those thoughts come from? Now those words tormented me.

A talent with character voices and dialects landed me a job with the First Amendment Comedy & Improvisation Company Off-Broadway where I was given the nickname "The Woman of 101 Voices." I did the one-woman performance "The Betty Boop Show" and appeared on television with the woman who did the original voices for Betty Boop and Popeye's Olive Oyl, Mae Questel. People said I was "the funniest woman they had ever seen."

While confident on-stage, I felt insecure off-stage. I continued on my search for inner peace and spiritual enlightenment. I practiced meditation, chanting, aura balancing, chakra cleansing, past life recall, psychism, and channeling. I visited shamans, psychics, sweat lodges, caves and shrines.

In addition to all these things, I studied bits and pieces from the Bible, but believed the Christian worldview was 'kindergarten' compared to the higher truths I imagined. I believed the answers I sought were just around the corner in the next conference, the next book, the next spiritual high. I was certain I was just one experience away from being the person I longed to be.

Before every new experience I felt hope and excitement. During each experience I felt closer than I had ever been before. I wanted a real, verifiable experience with God. "Maybe this is it!" I thought. But then afterwards I felt the let-down, and the emptiness returned. I felt like a donkey following a carrot dangling from a string placed in front of its nose. I continually sought the next spiritual experience, the next new teaching. Where was the God of my childhood?

You Can Always Return to Me

My mother had a little rhyme she would repeat from time-to-time when I was a child. As I sat on her lap, she'd hold me in her arms, gently rocking me and saying, "Travel the whole world over. Sail the deep blue sea. When your wanderlust is over, you can always return to me."

I wanted to travel the whole world over. I felt that if I were to visit some of the sacred sites I'd read about I would have a spiritual experience that would change me and I'd become the focused, confident, spiritually-enlightened person I longed to be.

In the mid-1980s my father became very ill with complications from heart disease and diabetes. I was grateful I could be with him in the hospital during the last weeks of his life. Even though Dad had not been to church in years, I learned that Father Palmer, who had been the priest at St. Thomas Episcopal Church, visited my father and prayed with him. That meant a lot to me, and I noticed that Dad was remarkably calmer the last week of his life. He didn't seem scared anymore or see fearsome apparitions. The man who could fly into a rage at the least provocation seemed peaceful for the first time in his life. It wasn't until years later that I realized what may have happened during Father Palmer's visit. Dad made his peace with God.

After Dad's passing, I was able to do the travel I'd wanted to do. I went to many of the world's sacred sites in Europe, the U.S. and Peru. I spent thousands of dollars and countless hours looking for

God and searching for enlightenment. At one spiritual conference, I was suddenly lifted thirty feet in the air looking down at the top of everyone's head—although physically my feet never left the floor. I felt giddy and elated for about 20 seconds, and then it was over. At an event in California a famous channeled entity challenged me when I said I had a "tremendous desire to serve people." The supposed Ascended Master scolded me in front of 1200 followers, "Serve thyself, entity!" I felt hurt. My high hopes of being my own god were dashed. "I'm hopeless," I thought.

I visited Stonehenge and Glastonbury in England, in search of mystical encounters. One morning I rose before dawn and climbed Chalice Hill in Glastonbury, overlooking the site of mythical Avalon of Arthurian legend, supposed resting place of the Holy Grail. Standing alone beside St. Michael's Tower, I looked out over the fog-laden valley. I felt no closer to God—or Camelot. I just felt alone.

In Scotland during a meditation, I astral projected out of my body, flipped over and was shocked to be nose-to-nose with my own serene self. Shocked, I fell back into my physical body. I saw visions, heard voices and had psychic abilities, yet felt empty inside—the carrot continually dangled in front of my nose as I sought God.

Sitting in a cave on a cliff in Crete overlooking the Mediterranean Sea I gazed at the sky looking for a sign, looking for God. "Where are You?" I asked.

The more I travelled, the more desperate I became to have an encounter that not only gave me a spiritual thrill, but provided both peace and inner fulfillment. After six months visiting dozens of sacred sites in twenty countries I felt agitated and hopeless. God was not to be found in these places.

I sought God in the spectacular. I wanted an earth-moving experience to prove to me He was real. I'm reminded what the angels said to Mary Magdalene and the other women who sought the body of Jesus at the tomb after His crucifixion. *"Why do you seek the living among the dead? He is not here, but is risen!"* (Luke 24:5-6). I discovered there are no sacred sites magnetized to hold God's presence. He's just not there. But the "image of God" who walked on the earth nearly 2000 years ago is "risen" and His Holy Spirit will also indwell all who ask Jesus to reside on the throne of their hearts and be Lord of their lives. But these mysteries were hidden from me then.

The spectacular experiences, while they thrilled me for the moment, left me empty, agitated, and craving another 'fix.' Later, after I accepted a relationship with the Person of Jesus Christ, I discovered that my encounters with God could be sweet, profound, fulfilling—and the deep sense of peace His presence engenders remains.

A Dangerous Question

After my parents died, I decided to leave a so-so career as an actor in New York City for the seeming serenity of a New Age community in the Ozark foothills. "I'll go where I'm happy and start my life over again," I thought. Since I didn't find God in my travels to sacred sites, I hoped settling in a community centered on a person channeling an Ascended Master would bring me closer to the source of enlightenment.

Not surprisingly, the change of scenery did not change *me*. As the saying goes, "Wherever you go, there *you* are." The empty feelings and unhappiness followed me from New York City.

I was lonely. I wanted someone to love me for myself. In the end, it was the loneliness that brought me to my knees.

The first time I surrendered to God was the most difficult thing I'd ever done. Control has always been important to me. No one likes feeling helpless. When I became aware of my mother's psychological weaknesses as a child, I remember clenching my fists and saying to myself, "I will never be weak. I will always be strong." It didn't work. I was a practicing alcoholic from the ages of thirteen to twenty-nine.

In the spring of 1987 I was driving home to the New Age community where I lived, when a 'dangerous' question entered my mind. **"What if everything you thought about God was completely wrong. Would you be willing to give it up to know the Truth?"**

That question was dangerous because it led me to doubt what I thought I knew. I had a lot invested in the New Age and yoga—twenty-two years of my life. I was even being groomed to play a role as one of the spiritual leaders in the community where I lived.

That question in my mind begged an answer. "What if everything you thought about God was completely wrong. Would you be willing to give it up to know the Truth?" "If" was a big word.

"If everything I thought about God was completely wrong," I said aloud. "Would I be willing to give it all up to know the truth?" Well, *if* I was wrong... "Yes," I answered. Yes, I would be willing to give up everything I thought I knew about God in order to know the truth.

The next day I came to the end of myself.

The April Fool?

On April 1st I was alone with my border collie Tula in my little house on the mountain. I walked in circles around the kitchen for what seemed like hours. I called out to God.

From the depths of my being I cried, "I surrender. I give up. You win. If you can do something with this life, You can have it." I knew I was crying out to the Jesus of my childhood. I asked Him to forgive me for making such a mess of my life.

Between sobs I said, "If You want me to be alone, then give me peace. If You want me to be with someone, then send him soon, because I can't live like this anymore."

I fell on my knees and then on my face. As I did, I felt a physical weight lift off me and something I'd never experienced before—peace like a dove came upon me and filled me. This peace was not the mind-numbing serenity I'd experienced during yoga meditations. It was not the blissful emptiness where nothing really mattered. I felt loved and embraced, accepted and fully, vibrantly alive.

The Peace I'd Been Missing

Peace. I'd never known how good it could feel. I never knew what peace was before. I'd always associated it with boredom or the words "Rest in Peace" on cartoon tombstones. This was different. From the center of this remarkable peace came joy. This joy I felt was not mere happiness or the giddy delight of opening presents. For the first time in my life I felt complete. Perhaps the best word for it is *shalom* in Hebrew—which means peace; wholeness; nothing missing, and nothing broken.

"For He Himself is our peace," the Apostle Paul wrote of Jesus in the New Testament (Ephesians 2:14). For me, His peace was the missing piece. I gave God everything I had, every mixed-up, messed-up part—and He gave me Himself: love, completeness and glorious, childlike joy.

The Jesus of my childhood, the One who laughed at my jokes was not a religion, but a Person. I never wanted to have a *religion*! I wanted a relationship—a relationship with God. That's what I'd been looking for all my life—to actually know God. I wanted to hear His voice, love Him—and know His love for me.

Oh, how I wished someone had told me sooner that I could have an actual relationship with God! Why did no one tell me that all the knowledge in the world could not equal one spark of revelation from God? By being willing to give up everything I thought I knew about God, I came to know the Truth. I learned that the Truth is not a debatable philosophy or mindset, but a Person: Jesus Christ. He said, *"I am the way, the <u>truth</u> and the life. No one comes to the Father except through Me"* (John 14:6).

That April Fool's Day I went from being a fool for the world, to a fool for Christ. I don't worry about looking or sounding foolish for sharing the love of Jesus. How I wish others had been willing to be that foolish when I was so lost and alone—imprisoned behind the wall of separation from God.

Shortly after I surrendered to God I realized I no longer had any desire to drink the bottles of Italian wine I used to consume on an almost daily basis since I was thirteen years old. The desire was completely gone. In God's great mercy, He removed alcoholism with the weight He lifted off me.

Remember the prayer I prayed, "If You want me to be alone, then give me peace. If You want me to be with someone, then send him soon…"? Four days later, I met Paul Willis, and we were married three months later, on the 4th of July 1987 and have celebrated twenty-six years of bliss this past year.

I discovered that God will give you the desires of your heart when you delight yourself in Him.

God's Sense of Humor

God has a sense of humor—and He never wastes a thing in our lives. The gifts and natural talents I had since childhood have come to fruition and found fulfillment in my relationship with Him.

One of the reasons I left the theater in New York City was because of the emptiness I felt. The applause no longer satisfied me. Since then I've been blessed to present a number of original theater performances through our company, DoveTale Productions. Remember how the 'Ascended Master' rebuked me for my desire to serve others? I've heard that the word 'entertainment' comes from a Latin word which means "to serve." Entertaining others felt empty for years, because I didn't feel I had anything worthwhile to share. Now I do. I no longer entertain to be served by others' handclaps and accolades, but because I finally have something meaningful to give.

Since 1993 I've presented one-woman shows and ensemble productions in theaters, schools, churches and community centers. I enjoy writing shows that bring history 'off the page' in interactive ways for today's audiences.

I've also been amazed that my years in yoga have not been wasted either. We started a Fitness Ministry called PraiseMoves in 2003, and now have DVDs and books with Harvest House Publishers, two television shows for children and adults seen by over 250 million people globally, and Certified PraiseMoves Instructors on four continents bringing a Christ-centered alternative to yoga to communities around the world. Our website www.praisemoves.com has drawn millions of visitors.

Over 125 postures are each linked to a different verse from the Bible, as well as numerous "Scripture Sequences:" multiple postures that coincide with quoting longer passages like the 23rd Psalm or the Lord's Prayer.

Actually, I believe that physical exercise is not the foundation to PraiseMoves. The Scripture we meditate upon is the foundation. The exercise is the "witty invention" to get us more into the Word of God from the Bible, and to get more of the Word into us—hence our slogan, "Transform your workouts into worship" with PraiseMoves.

We even have a series of postures based on the shapes and meanings of the letters in the Hebrew alphabet (*alef-bet*). I studied the Kabbalah in the New Age, but this teaching is different—everything points to Jesus as Messiah! For example, the Hebrew word for religion is "*dat*," which is a combination of the fourth letter of the alphabet *dalet* (which means "door") and the 22nd letter *tav* (which originally looked like a cross, or the lower case letter 't'—and held the meaning of "sign" or "cross"). So, the ancient Hebrew word for religion is "door of the cross." How remarkable is that?

The Center of My Joy

I thank God I found "the door of the cross" and walked through it. As I look back, I am grateful beyond words that I did not lose my life during one of the many alcoholic blackouts I had in my teens and twenties. I didn't lose my mind while dabbling in the supernatural, dallying in the psychic arena as if it were a sandbox; allowing my body to be used as a channel for strange spiritual forces, instead of a vessel yielded to God.

The God who laughed at my jokes and comforted me in the darkness of my closet has become the center of peace and light within my own heart. He has become the center of my joy! I would have never imagined that all the love, peace, wisdom and spiritual fulfillment I craved could be found in relationship with Jesus, the God of the Bible, the Living Word and Creator of the universe.

One day the Author of Love asked me a question, "What if everything you thought about God was completely wrong. Would you be willing to give it up to know the Truth?" I'm glad I answered yes to the Truth. How about you? What if...?

Laurette Willis is the founder/director of PraiseMoves, a popular, biblically based alternative to yoga. She has two PraiseMoves telecasts (one for children and one for adults) seen by a potential audience of over 250 million people globally, as well as certified PraiseMoves.

Chapter 8

WITCHCRAFT TO GOD'S WARRIOR

By Gary

By the age of twelve, I was living with my father, smoking marijuana and Marlboro Reds, while cruising for willing girls every chance I could. Dad kept us in church every Easter and Christmas, quoted Corinthians every time his wife disagreed with him, and ruled his house with an iron fist. During the day, my brother and I would play 'Dungeons and Dragons' to get away from the emotional and physical abuse, leading to an addiction of running from reality through fantasy that would last for years. At night I would sneak downstairs to watch the Playboy channel while everyone else slept.

The summer I turned thirteen my mother received custody of me and my younger sister, splitting the three children up. It was a horrific time of lies and deceptions as both Mom and Dad used every means at their disposal to hurt the other through us kids. When the dust settled, I was in Texas with my mother and didn't speak to my Dad again for two years.

It was July when a local neighbor kid approached me about something called 'VBS'. Little did I know what was going on when I rode with him to a church near our house. A large group of kids were there, and we played, ate, and sang songs I had never heard before. As the day drew to a close, one of the adults came into the room where we were all seated and began to tell the story of Jesus. By the point of the crucifixion I was in tears. I remember being led into another room to say a prayer. ***The only thing I remember about that event was asking Jesus to come into my heart.*** Someone gave me a bible and I started to read.

My mother had no interest in being a part of my new life. My step-father made it clear that if I wanted to attend a church that it was my business. He, on the other hand, would have none of it in his house. So I attended by myself in my yard sale clothes, with my 'poor white trash' lifestyle, and started to learn how to love God. I became very hungry for the Word of God but when I went to Sunday school and asked so many questions I was told to be quite.

The church had a small private school and every Sunday the Pastor would petition the congregation for more money to keep the school open and it did. One Sunday morning, the lesson was on the world, and how things were going in it. That morning, my whole hope of salvation was dashed with the words, ***"If your kids are in a public school instead of our private school, you are sending them to Hell."*** I knew that there was no way my parents would find the money to send me to this private school so in my thirteen year old logic, I made the decision that if I was going to Hell anyhow, I might as well make the best of it. And so I did....

Like most teenagers, I spent most of my time thinking about the opposite sex. The biggest difference between me and 'them' was the single-mindedness I had concerning sex. It was all I could think about, and thoughts of perversion dominated my mind. I found myself getting interested in every depraved and ungodly act I could find. In the midst of all this, I met a girl who would have nothing to do with me. I became completely obsessed with her, and determined in my mind that I would do anything to get her.

Sin is a magnet to other sinners, and in this case, a powerful one. I met another girl in school who claimed to be a witch. She explained that she could perform a spell for me that would absolutely get me the girl I wanted. I did all the things she required of me, and within three weeks the girl was mine.

Immediately I was no longer interested in the girl, sex or drugs but this 'power' that could change the very desires of men. I thought, *"If I could master something like this, no one would be able to hurt me ever again."* Every available moment was spent digging into books and articles about witchcraft. I wanted to understand it, use it and master it. Little did I see that it began to master me.

Within one year while I was in my Junior year of High School, I felt like I was getting good at "The Craft" and discovered the science of Demonology. I dove headlong into this discipline, buying books, attending ceremonies and absorbing everything I could get my hands on. I began to discern the difference between charlatans and real demons. And for once, I began to fear. I began to see that Hell is for real and that demons can possess people, and could kill them at will.

A young man introduced me to a particularly demonic tome full of spells and curses. He warned me that after reading this book, he had begun to have terrifying nightmares and could hear demons talking to him at night. Skeptically, I began studying and practicing some of the spells myself. All that came to a halt within a month when this same young man was arrested for attempting to kill his mother with a kitchen knife. I spoke to him later, and he shared with me that he had been wrestling with the demons who kept telling him to kill his mother. The night of the attack he said that he lost consciousness and had no recollection of the events whatsoever. While the legal and medical fields dismissed this as a mental health issue, I knew better. Now I was gripped with fear and wanted to learn how to protect myself and gain mastery over these invisible forces.

After graduation, I moved to Georgia to live with my father and to escape the dominion of my mother. There were also some of the most powerful cults in America in the Atlanta area. I immediately linked into a group of Wiccans that taught me how to read Tarot cards, how to release my spirit from my body through what is known as Astral projection, and a variety of curses and blessings that I could command. At last, I found people who were convinced they could command and control the demonic forces I had already seen in action. But they were so wrong. Rather than control these forces, they were used by them to seduce others into this deception. With each passing hour, we sought deeper and deeper extremes of depravity and power.

My life continued to slide into decadence and depravity. Every new experience was to be desired and every taboo to be explored. Each day found me looking for something new to try. I began reading books about Satanic worship and Hedonism. I left the perceived safety of witchcraft and began going even deeper into Hell. By the time the summer ended, I had found the writings of a man who taught Satanic worship without the distasteful sacrifice of children and animals. Instead, he glorified the flesh while acknowledging the need of man for spiritual food. His arguments were compelling, and sinfully delicious. As an 18 year old male, with no meaningful discipline in his life, all this fit in quite nicely with the desires I spent every evening fulfilling.

I started to become bored and decided that what I needed was another change in my life so I enlisted in the military and was shipped out in 1989. While in basic training, I remembered someone I had left behind several years ago.

One aspect of basic training is the Sunday morning service to help new soldiers adjust to their new lifestyles. It is not mandatory to attend but if you don't, you can stay behind and clean the dorms and for this reason, you can understand why they are so popular. It was because of this need for a break that I found myself walking into a church. It seemed silly to me, almost ironic, that a servant of Satan could walk into this sanctuary in sheep's clothing. I couldn't explain the pit in my stomach, so I dismissed it as breakfast. But sometime during the choir's singing of "Amazing Grace", conviction washed over me and I found myself on my knees, begging God to have mercy on me. All the scriptures I had forgotten came rushing back in like tidal waves.

For the remainder of Basic Training, I was faithful to attend church every Sunday, but because I had no Christian support system in place, as soon as I was released back into the world I went back to the vomit I knew.

Over the next seven years, my life fell into a slide of hate and misery. My self-esteem fell to a point where suicide was not an "if" but a "how" and turned to alcohol to dull the emptiness in my life.

I married a girl from the area where I was stationed, and promptly began to ruin her life as well. Neither of us had any kind of spiritual foundation to base a marriage on. Instead we floundered through the days trying every pop psychological idea that was hot at the time. I introduced her to all the mysticism that I had learned over the years, and together we searched desperately for meaning and purpose in life.

A long season of financial strain, spiritual darkness, and relational ups and downs nearly ended our marriage. Just before we were to separate, however, Tina became excited about a new business opportunity – one that I, too, became curious about.

I went to a meeting with her to check it out and just as I had thought, it was an Amway meeting. But unlike the other times I had been to one of these things, this time seemed different. Intrigued by this feeling, I agreed to check things out and attend their upcoming convention. The money wasn't there for one of us to go, let alone both, but somehow I ended up going. I knew that many of the folks were Christians, and suspected that there would be plenty of brainwashing going on. I also assumed that my mind was girded up enough to keep me from making any emotional decisions.

The convention was three days long with a Sunday morning service taking place before the wrap up speakers. During that service, the Holy Spirit came back to visit. I was standing in respect of those around me, when an understanding of Jesus' death came into my mind. I saw Him hanging on the cross, His blood flowing. I felt the wall around my heart shatter, and ran to the floor of the arena to join the altar call. On July 7, 1996 I made a decision that stuck. This time, supported by a family of believers that helped me grow and understand, the decision was backed by more than just tears. I now had a support network that I could ask questions of, and fall back to when things got hard.

And the son said unto him, Father, I have sinned against heaven, and in thy sight, and am no more worthy to be called thy son. But the father said to his servants, Bring forth the best robe, and put it on him; and put a ring on his hand, and shoes on his feet: And bring hither the fatted calf, and kill it; and let us eat, and be merry: For this my son was dead, and is alive again; he was lost, and is found. And they began to be merry.

Luke 15:21-24 (KJV)

Giving my life to Christ during the convention did not make all my problems go away. There would be many years of sanctification, transformation, and deep healing to come for both my wife and myself. But the direction of our lives was definitely new. My heart was now in the hands of my Heavenly Father instead of in the clutches of the father of lies. Years of Christian relationships and godly wisdom through church fellowship continue to change my life. I've most definitely come a long way since my days of tarot cards and witchcraft.

I was praying one day about the pain of being so broken and of the suffering and turmoil that my life as one of "God's Warriors" has brought. The Lord showed me a vision that day of a beautiful pedestal that held two vases. The first vase was perfect, with delicate unbroken curves and intricate colors painted in magnificent patterns. I saw oil being poured into this vase until it was completely full. The oil licked at the edges at the top of the vase, but none spilled out.

The second vase was the opposite of the first. It had obviously been dropped and broken at some point, and while it had been glued back together there were pieces missing and excess glue flowed from the cracks. As I saw the oil about to be poured into this shattered vessel I already knew that the oil would go to waste as the vase would not be able to contain it. However, as I watched the expected results take place, I saw for the first time that many other vases were arranged around the base of the pedestal! As the oil flowed through the cracks and holes of the broken vase it filled the others as well!

The Lord said to me that day, *"You are that broken vase. The other vase, though perfect to look at, can only be filled with enough oil for itself. After that, the oil it has is all it will ever know. But you, in your brokenness, will not only share the oil that flows through you... BUT you will also see never ending streams of fresh oil as you will never be full. I did not cause you to be broken, but I did cause you to be healed. I did not restore you to what you were before your brokenness, but rather for the brokenness to remake you into something greater."*

Chapter 9

UNCONDITIONAL LOVE

By Rosemary

As a girl growing up I struggled with the concept of unconditional love or even the idea of a heavenly Father who loved me with all my flaws, hang ups and bad habits. The reason I struggled to believe was because my "earthly" father modeled the exact opposite. I never heard my father tell me that he loved me, that I was beautiful or worth fighting for. My father never expressed any interest at all in learning what my gifts were or what made my heart sing.

My father was the problem parent who always engaged in some form of immature, inappropriate, or destructive behavior which was a detriment to our entire family. He drank daily (unless he had a major hangover), used foul language, and physically and mentally abused my mother and our entire family due to his alcoholic addiction and fits of rage and anger. This did not happen on occasion but for the majority of my childhood.

My mother, on the other hand, was a passive parent who allowed this inappropriate behavior to continue, which always left me and my older brother in dangerous situations. Her self-esteem and self-worth were so low that she continuously allowed my father to break her down and control and manipulate her to believe that it was all her fault for the broken relationship and violence within our family.

I witnessed the love my mother would put forth to please my father, and because she would not stick up for herself or protect us from my father, I grew to despise and resent her weakness as a woman. This was when the trouble began in my spirit. I began making silent vows within my soul to NEVER allow a man to control my life, like my father controlled her and our family.

Although my family life was a mess, I had no choice but to grow accustomed to the constant chaos. I loved both of my parents and wanted nothing more than to have a "happy" home life. It was my heartbeat and desire to be loved and for them to love each other. I would continue to pray and wish that one day I would hear those precious words to every story I read as a little girl..."and they lived happily ever after".

Mother took us to church and did her best to instill spiritual beliefs in us. Unfortunately, my father was aligned with a different church with conflicting theology that caused more confusing competition. I was in love with God and wanted Him to love me back by protecting me. I wanted God to rescue me and my family from all the pain our family was enduring and was willing to do whatever God wanted me to do to fix this.

The more I jumped on my father's back to release my mother or my brother from my father's clutches, the more scared, insecure and angry I became. I continued to resent my mother's weakness for not leaving, and my brother vented his anger on me and vice versa. Not only did I feel resentment toward my mother but I began questioning the validity of our church as well. Along with gossip about our family, was a passive resignation toward the black eyes my Mother often wore on Sundays. And another thing: Why was I hearing what the Bible taught about certain behaviors and then seeing the church folks acting in opposite ways during the week? What kind of religion is that? Not anything I wanted. I wanted REAL!

I was nine years old when my father died suddenly on his thirty-third birthday. He was fatally hit by a tractor-trailer full of his favorite comfort drink: beer. To his credit, my mother was able to sustain our lifestyle after his death because he had always been a wonderful provider in a material way.

His funeral was my first, and as the casket lowered into the ground, the finality of things hit me hard. He was gone. It was over, and I would never have a chance to hear from his lips that I was loved, beautiful, captivating and worth fighting for. I was broken not knowing how to pick up the pieces. Only later in life did I understand that he had no idea how to love his family or to share his heart. His father had acted the same toward his family, a repeated pattern that became a generational curse.

We were now free from the physical and verbal abuse, but the freedom mentality also brought much destruction along with it. Since my mother hated the control that my father had on her and our family, she thought it was best to make it up to me by not having any boundaries on my life that left me wide open to do what I wanted and when I wanted. I lost all respect for authority and stepped into the role of being my own authority since my mother relinquished her responsibility. I quit school in the eighth grade and got involved with a rough crowd in our neighborhood.

Over a short period, I lost interest in being a fourteen-year-old honor roll student who was active in sports and horseback riding and decided to hang out in bars with my mother was more important than my grades or sports. Church had to go, too. What use were those who put on a big front once a week, only to become someone different during the week? My friends would at least be real and genuine, even if their lives were a mess. A new disgust for church and all it stood for had settled deep within my heart.

As my mother continued her "party" lifestyle, she became extremely depressed and soon after my sixteenth birthday; she committed suicide and left me and my brother to fend for ourselves. She believed that I was strong enough to handle life on my own and did not need her anymore. We were devastated.

The shock of finding her dead only intensified my disbelief that there was a God that was loving and kind. The only person who I trusted that loved me chose to leave me. Not for a little while, but forever! The memory of trying to bring her back to life and to beg her not to leave me seems as if it was yesterday. The thought of it being my fault would replay over and over in my heart and mind.

Why did I leave her and start hanging out with other girlfriends? Why didn't I hang out more at home? Why didn't I watch her more carefully? Why did I treat her with such disrespect? Why? Why? Why? The only cure for the constant battle within my mind was to kill the pain and voices with alcohol and bad relationships.

The day she died, her "religious" family came over to claim what they thought was theirs. While sitting in my living room chair in shock over her death praying that I would wake up to discover that I was in a bad nightmare, I could hear her family in the kitchen talking among each other saying "Mary told me I could have this... Mary told me I could have that." As I continued to hear them casting lots for my mother's belongings, the anger festered within my entire being to the point of chasing each one of them out of our home.

Because of not having a "healthy," "secure" or "protective" environment, I didn't know how to have healthy relationships with my family, friends or people in authority. I was impaired emotionally, psychologically and spiritually. I continued to have false ideas of who God was, and the enemy was ready and willing to feed me plenty of lies along the way. Remember, I made internal vows never to trust a man or allow a man to control my life, and this is when the rebellion began to bear fruit in my life.

With no one left to count on, no one anywhere worthy of my trust, the thing left to do was to run and kill the pain with alcohol, drugs and lethal relationships. Looking back, I was becoming everything I hated. I was turning into my father in spite of vowing years earlier that I would NEVER act like him.

A current pop song on the radio was, "Running with the Devil." The enemy used the power of music as an invitation to give my life to him and to lose my faith in a loving God. As the song played I announced, "If God is so mean to take away everything I love... I would rather run with the devil!" That day I opened the door for my life to become a living hell.

And run with the devil I did --- with a hell-bent mission to crash and burn in a flame of glory. After years of drinking, drug use, sick relationships and a failed marriage, I lost all desire to continue on until I met a very special friend. A friend who loved me more than my mother ever knew how.

Her name was Christine, and we were introduced by a mutual business contact that knew we would work well together because Chris was a clothing designer, and I had a modeling agency. We were instant friends and God with His divine wisdom knew she was the only woman who could run with me that I would respect because of her strength and her talents that overshadowed mine. She immediately took the lead role as my older sister, sticking with me through my wild escapades and off-the-edge drinking bouts. She also witnessed my first time falling in love with a man I knew was too good for me.

Well versed in the disease of alcoholism due to family involvement, she easily recognized what I wanted to hide. Alcohol was my master; I had no power to overcome the addiction or had a replacement to cover the pain that was so deep ingrained within my heart and soul. But Chris had seen the other side of the alcohol story. She knew there were deliverance and healing --- from the proper source. The moment of truth came on a long drive home one night when she turned to me with teary eyes, announcing, "If you don't stop this lifestyle, you are going to die, and I can't watch it anymore. I love and care about you, and either you allow me to get you help or you will need to find another business partner and friend. I can no longer watch you destroy yourself."

When Chris spoke, she delivered. A "mover and a shaker" type, she got things done ... and she meant business. I understood the challenge: Allow my best friend to get me meaningful help, or lose her forever. What kind of love this was --- or where it originated I could not imagine. With a melted heart, I was ready because, for the first time in my life, I had someone who loved me enough to tell me the truth.

I never experienced someone truly concerned about my welfare or well being. She was the first friend I ever had that was willing to be that voice to speak the truth into my life in hopes that I would choose life instead of death.

The next day Chris picked me up and took me to my first Alcoholics Anonymous (AA) meeting. It was a strange and scary door to walk through. It was a Holy Spirit door where He began the work on my heart and in my life.

God knew I was adamant about not stepping foot back into the church because of those hypocrites. So God sent me where I needed to go, and He was ever so present because where His people are, so is He.

While I attended AA meetings, I heard testimonies of people just like me. People who even did worse things than I did, yet they were happy, free and full of life! I noticed that they all had something in common that I did not have. They had "Jesus" as their Higher Power and were in "relationship" with Him. I thought...Jesus! Jesus as a Higher Power?

This wasn't any kind of Christianity I'd ever heard of. And this wasn't the Jesus I understood from childhood. In my thinking, God and Jesus were mean-spirited dictators who could never be pleased. I was always on the wrong side of them. They were like my father, unpredictable and impossible to please. Right?

Wrong! I knew my problems were bigger than I was, and it was either going to be life or death for me. I knew I could not fix myself because I tried every "new age" belief system, "self-help guru" and bought books and tapes on positive thinking and meditation. It would work for a short period only to find myself back once again in the pit of Hell repeating old habits and self-sabotaging behaviors.

Although I made a committed vow never to darken the church doors again, it was no accident that all of the AA meetings were held in church basements or sanctuaries. Ironically, after experiencing God's love through other people and having found hope of the many testimonies I heard of a new-found freedom, I would find myself many times trying to find a church that was open during off hours just to get in to seek who God was and try to find Him. I reached a point where the doors were locked at so many churches that I would hang on the door, asking God to let the sinner in!

I wish I could tell you that I had a perfect scorecard for sobriety in the beginning and that I did not have to start over a few times because of relapsing. Those failures were lessons that taught me how desperately I needed a Savior that possessed the power that I did not have. It was that day that forever changed my life when I surrendered and dedicated my life to Christ Jesus as my Lord and Savior.

I will forever cherish that day when falling on my knees on my living room floor that I cried out to the Lord for His help and to save me. I told Him I no longer wanted to live this way, and I was completely powerless over my life and situation. With a broken and contrite heart, a healing peace enveloped my entire spirit right then and there. With His forgiveness, I began an inner transformation, like moving from the dark cocoon of a caterpillar to the freedom of a soaring butterfly! On that day, everything looked brighter, like blinders had fallen from my eyes. I became hungry for truth, hungry to live, hungry to take responsibility for my choices and most of all a hunger to get to know and have a personal relationship with my heavenly Father.

God sent my best friend Christine to love me until I learned to love myself. He sent Christine to speak the truth into my life with love and concern. He sent Christine to set the example of how Christians are to serve others and how we are to love one another that draws them to Christ Jesus, not repels them. He used her love and concern to draw me into His loving arms and back to His church.

Yes, I am back in church, but for totally different reasons. I am no longer focused on taking everyone's inventory but concerned with what Jesus will say to me when I see Him face to face. He will not ask me about others, but will ask me what I have done for His kingdom. I come to church to worship my heavenly Father, to fellowship and learn the Word of God so I can live it and help others. It is my desire to love "unconditionally" as Christ loved me and how Christine showed me in the flesh. I always have to remind myself that no church denomination is perfect and that the church will always be filled with hurting people who are looking for the Christine's with Christ in them to serve them, love them where they are at and hear true testimonies of how God worked in their lives to give them hope for their futures.

God truly is a redeemer, restorer and repairer of damaged lives and circumstances. I made a choice to follow God and renounced the stronghold that the devil had on my life by the choice I made. I repented and have been forgiven. I have many stories and scars to show the destructive life that I led for many years that would take up this entire book. I have a testimony of what a mess looks like that is no different than yours. A mess is a mess regardless of how big or small it is. By God's grace, I chose to come to Him and received His spirit for a new life. My lost childhood, deceased parents and lifestyle scars all bear witness that He was who I needed all along. He is who my entire family needed, even the very religious ones. God has walked me through layers of forgiveness toward my father, my mother and myself. He walked me through laying down the old and taking up the new.

By the way, that man I fell in love with (the one I thought was too good for me) became my husband more than eighteen years ago. We serve Jesus Christ together as best friends. We have an incredible sixteen-year-old son who is blessed to live in a Christ-centered home where love and respect prevail. He knows we are not perfect, but that we are the same inside and outside our home.

I started a speaking ministry that was founded by God but given to me to lead women to share their stories of transformation and to challenge them to find God's very best for their lives. I pray that one day you will find joy in telling your story so that you can give God all the glory for His work of grace in you.

It is never too late! God is available and willing to intercede at any time to help you. Never forget that it does not matter how we begin, it only matters how we finish.

This is my personal testimony and as a "Rapture Ready" Bride and the author of this book, I invite you to lay down the past and start a new, vibrant and loving relationship with your Creator. Whether you were like me and spent years in church but never asked Jesus Christ with a sincere heart to be your Lord and Savior; or perhaps you have backslidden and need to repent and get right with God, don't you think it is time to give up an ordinary life for an extraordinary life with eternal benefits? I do and I believe in you and am praying for you!

Therefore, if anyone is in Christ, he is a new creation; old things have passed away; behold, all things have become new.

2 Corinthians 5:17 (NKJV)

Rosemary is the author of the Smokin' "HOT" Bride of Christ and Broken Hearts Have No Color. For more information on her speaking ministry and Bride of Christ conferences, please visit www.rosemaryfisher.com

Chapter 10

COMMITMENT TO CHRIST

Living an Exciting *"Rapture Ready"* Life Begins with Salvation

My prayer is that these stories touched you in such a powerful way that you have a strong desire to have a passionate relationship with your Lord and Savior. It does not matter where you are at in life right now, it only matters how you finish. I encourage you to finish well and become *"Rapture Ready"* for God's glory!

Today you can surrender your old life for an extraordinary life! There are no hidden tricks or agendas. All that is needed is a sincere and willing heart! God wants you to receive His gift of salvation through His Son, Jesus Christ. Are you ready? If so… let's pray….

Father, You loved the world so much You gave Your only begotten Son to die for our sins so that whoever believes in Him will not perish, but have eternal life. Your Word says we are saved by grace through faith as a gift from You and there is nothing we can do to earn salvation.

I believe in my heart and confess with my mouth that Jesus Christ is Your Son, My Savior and the Savior of the world. I believe He died on the cross, bore all of my sins and You raised Him from the dead.

I confess Jesus as my Lord and Savior and ask that you forgive my sins and fill me up with Your Holy Spirit. Thank you for loving me enough to give Your very best for my salvation. In Jesus' holy name, I pray AMEN!!

The transformation begins right here! You have been given the gift of eternal life, and the Spirit of Christ Jesus is residing in your heart!

Ask the Holy Spirit to help you find a church that teaches the Word of God so you can learn and grow. Also find a women's bible study to meet other Christian sisters to help you along the way. Don't be shy! True Sisters of Christ want to celebrate with you and will welcome you with open arms! If that does not happen, keep moving until you find a place where God wants you to be.

It is important for you to understand that it takes awhile to get what the inside has on the outside, so be patient and partner with God by reading and studying the Holy Bible as He begins to transform you from a caterpillar into a beautiful butterfly!

If this book has touched your heart in anyway, please share your story by sending me an email at rosemary@rosemaryfisher.com. I would love to hear from you.

Scriptures:

John 3:16 (NIV)
For God so loved the world that he gave his one and only Son, that whoever believes in him shall not perish but have eternal life.

Ephesians 2:8-9 (NIV)
For it is by grace you have been saved, through faith—and this is not from yourselves, it is the gift of God— not by works, so that no one can boast.

Romans 10:9-10 (NIV)
If you declare with your mouth, "Jesus is Lord," and believe in your heart that God raised him from the dead, you will be saved. For it is with your heart that you believe and are justified, and it is with your mouth that you profess your faith and are saved.

1 Corinthians 15:3-4 (NLT)
I passed on to you what was most important and what had also been passed on to

me. Christ died for our sins, just as the Scriptures said. [4] *He was buried, and he was raised from the dead on the third day, just as the Scriptures said.*

1 John 1:9 (NKJV)
If we confess our sins, He is faithful and just to forgive us our sins and to cleanse us from all unrighteousness.

1 John 4:14-16 (NLT)
Furthermore, we have seen with our own eyes and now testify that the Father sent his Son to be the Savior of the world. All who confess that Jesus is the Son of God have God living in them, and they live in God. We know how much God loves us, and we have put our trust in his love. God is love, and all who live in love live in God, and God lives in them.

1 John 5:1 (NIV)
Everyone who believes that Jesus is the Christ is born of God, and everyone who loves the father loves his child as well.

1 John 5:12 (NIV)
Whoever has the Son has life; whoever does not have the Son of God does not have life.

1 John 5:13 (NIV)
I write these things to you who believe in the name of the Son of God so that you may know that you have eternal life.

INTRODUCTION TO BIBLE STUDY

I want to introduce you to a very special and anointed woman who recently came into my life. There is no doubt that meeting her was divinely orchestrated by the hand of God. Her name is Sheryl Pellatiro, and she is the founder of Solid Truth Ministries.

It is with great pleasure that I can bring to you a small portion of her anointed work – a study on how to become Rapture Ready. Before we begin, I feel it's important to share with you how this happened because ONLY God could bring to fruition something so beautiful.

I came across Sheryl's Bible study while I was doing final touches on *this* manuscript, and was in the middle of working through a different Bible study. Although I knew I was finished writing this book, I felt in my heart that something was missing and God had the answer.

As I began sharing the Smokin' "HOT" Bride of Christ message at women's conferences, ministry leaders would often ask if I had a Bible study to accompany it. Soon after, the Lord quickened my spirit, and I knew that a Bible study *must* accompany this book.

Soon, the Holy Spirit began to nudge my spirit about writing a Bible study. As I began my research, I came across Sheryl's study on The Bride of Christ. Immediately, I was mesmerized and I couldn't put it down.

I found her heart for God and His Bride intriguing. But mostly, I loved the strong biblical foundation in her writing. I contacted her and since that day, we've begun a wonderful friendship. Sheryl and I connected immediately and our passion for the urgency of getting God's message out and helping His people become Rapture Ready was evident. No doubt, God has begun a fabulous partnership.

While initially I believed God was calling *me* to write the Bible study, both Sheryl and I know that God orchestrated us to meet to use what was already written. There is no doubt that Father God put us together at such a time as this to prepare His Bride for His glorious return through this book and her Bible study.

Bible study is a *must* for every Believer! It is our prayer that you become so hungry for God's word that you cannot go a day without it.

This 5-day study is thorough, biblically sound, and it gives every Christian the personal and spiritual security of knowing what is in store for their eternal future. You are going to LOVE it!

The section of the Bible study in this book is just a small portion of the feast that awaits you in Sheryl's complete Bible study titled "The Bride of Christ ~ Becoming Rapture Ready," which can be purchased at www.solidtruthministries.com or on Amazon.com.

I know you will enjoy it as much as I have, and I pray it makes you want more and more of His Word. I love you all dearly. Now, it's time for you to meet Sheryl!

Rosemary Fisher

The Bride of Christ Rapture Ready Bible Study

By Sheryl Pallatiro

Precious One,

I've been writing and teaching Bible studies for over twenty years. Several years ago, as I contemplated the next study I was to write, I felt led to write a study on some of the end-time events. In thinking about this topic, I knew I was to approach it in a different manner. I've always been intrigued by the title God has given to the Church: *"The Bride of Christ"*. So I began to research the ancient Jewish wedding customs and how they relate to Christ's Bride, His Church. I became so excited the more I studied.

One of the important things that popped up in my research is that we, as Christ's Bride, are to get ourselves ready. We read in Revelation 19:7: *"Let us rejoice and be glad and give him the glory! For the wedding of the Lamb has come, and his bride has made herself ready."* What a wedding that will be! And I must say that *"The Bride of Christ: Becoming Rapture Ready"* Bible study has become one of my most popular ones. I believe it's because God is preparing His people and they love to think about what's ahead on the horizon ~ what God has planned for them.

I learned so much from this study and it has been a privilege sharing it with so many. I began to pray that God would give me a partner – someone who was also passionate about helping believers get ready. Then one day, I saw that one of my Facebook friends, Rosemary Fisher, had written a book called *"The Smokin' "HOT" Bride of Christ, Exchanging Regrets for Rewards Before His Return"* which is about preparing your mind, body and spirit for Christ's glorious return. I began to follow her more closely and eventually asked her for a copy of her book. In turn, I sent her my Bible study. It seemed that God was moving in both our hearts about this very topic. We soon talked on the phone and began a partnership to bring God's message of being Rapture Ready to the Church. Rosemary wrote the book about the serious condition of the church today and I have the bible study that will walk you through the biblical teachings of what is in store for His bride in the future. We both agreed we needed to make it a book set, so every new or mature believer in Christ could learn how significant and glorious event we are all to partake in together hopefully in the near future.

As a gift, I have enclosed a chapter from my bible study that both Rosemary and I believe is perfect for her book. We believe that Bible study is imperative to our growth and to feed on the Word of God and want to encourage you to purchase the entire Bible study to further your knowledge of all the wonderful things our Father has in store for His daughters.

God has the end written! This is His message, not ours. And it is privilege to share with you what God is teaching us, what God is showing us as we listen to Him and wait on Him to move us to the next place. Thank you for partnering with us!

In Christ,

Sheryl Pellatiro
www.solidtruthministries.org

BEING READY

The year-long separation period for the Jewish bride was anything but easy. In addition to the excitement welling up inside her, she also had many responsibilities. She needed to be ready—prepared—when her groom showed up. She did not want to be caught off guard. I doubt a day went by when she didn't think about the moment her groom would whisk her away. Her life changed the instant she accepted the bridal payment —the second she said "yes." She was no longer just a simple village girl with little responsibility. As an engaged young woman, she must now make plans for her future. Overnight, this Jewish maiden transformed into a responsible adult.

Once you and I accepted our Bridegroom's bridal payment, we too began a new journey. Entering into a covenant with Him offered us awesome privileges, but it also meant great responsibilities. We know that our Groom will return one day for us and the Bible tells us we need to be ready. We do not want to be caught unprepared. Jesus said, **"Be dressed ready for service and keep your lamps burning" (Luke 12:35).** In other words, He is telling us to be ready because His return is not far off. And it may be sooner than we expect.

This week, we will tackle the subject of "being ready." The topics we discuss are vital for every believer. I pray you and I will be equipped with knowledge about the *end times* and the practical biblical truths necessary to ready us for our Groom's appearance

Day 1

A VIRGIN BRIDE

Ask God to speak to your heart and show you His truth.

The key verse for today is **2 Corinthians 11:2**. Please write out this verse.

Today we approach a topic many believers often disregard because of the liberated world we live in. Regardless, I believe God laid out His commands for at least a couple reasons: first, to protect us, and second, to help us be ready for a future event.

Day 1 of Week 3, we observed that when Jesus was on earth—the home of His Bride—He paid a lofty price for her. Once the pledge was made, the Church became exclusively His. Today, we will consider this matter a little more. Hang in there with me as we discuss *purity*, how it applies to our lives now, and how it will be significant for that future wedding day.

We now continue with our ancient Jewish wedding customs. (Purchase the complete study for Ancient Jewish customs 1 – 8 at www.solidtruthministries.com)

Ancient custom #9:
The bride was to keep herself pure during the separation.

Throughout our study, we have discovered that the ancient bride was to prepare herself for her upcoming nuptials. On Day 5 of Week 3, we looked at how she would use the time of separation to prepare her garments. **Revelation 19:8** tells us that our righteous acts will be the garments *we* wear on our eternal wedding day. Another important way the ancient bride would be ready for her wedding was to stay pure throughout the betrothal. Engaging in sinful acts would only bring dishonor to her future husband and would certainly be offensive to the God of her people, not to mention going against the Jewish law. There were no intimate relations between the bride and groom before their big day. On her wedding day, it was critical that this Jewish girl present herself to her husband as a chaste and undefiled bride.

I love to see young people wearing "purity" rings. Wearing this ring is a reminder of the vow they made to God — and to themselves —to stay pure until the day they are married. If they are successful at fulfilling this vow, the bride and/or groom present to each other a beautiful gift. And no doubt, God is proud of them and will honor this commitment. Of course, teachers, professors, medical professionals, the media, and other sources around our world, preach that remaining a virgin is impossible and unrealistic. God's Word begs to differ. My message to young people is that even if they made mistakes in the past, they can start from this point forward and strive for purity. God will honor this commitment as He erases all our confessed sin (**1 John 1:9**).

Let's begin by traveling back to the Old Testament to understand more about God and His people—His nation. We will begin by observing portions of **Ezekiel 16**. *Note*: as an optional exercise, you may want to read Chapter 16 in its entirety.

From **Ezekiel 16**, read the following sections and summarize briefly:

Verses 1-5:

Verses 6-8:

Verses 9-14:

Verses 15-16; 32:

What word does God use to describe Israel, based on **verse 32**?

Remember, the people of God were often reminded of the commands Moses had carved out on stone tablets **(Exodus 20:1-17)**. What did God reveal about Himself to Moses as part of the Ten Commandments, based on **Exodus 20:5**? Fill in the blank:

"You shall not bow down to them or worship them; for I, the LORD your God, am a _____ God..."

From the earliest of days, God declared to His people that He wanted them all to Himself. He longed for an exclusive relationship with those He chose out of other nations, and those He loved above all else. Thus, God required total loyalty and devotion to Him *alone*. He was their God and they were His people. Centuries passed from that mountaintop encounter between God and Moses and by the time we read Ezekiel's words, it seems God's grief was clearly evident. He had done so much for His beloved ones, and they repaid Him by bowing down to foreign idols. They slapped Him in the face again and again. How His heart must have been utterly broken.

In our **Ezekiel** passage, God spills His heart to them: **"I spread the corner of my garment over you and covered your nakedness. I gave you my solemn oath and entered into a covenant with you...and you became mine...I bathed you with water...put** ointments on you. I clothed you...I dressed you...I adorned you with jewelry" (Ezekiel 16:8-10). And what did they do in return? They bowed to others. They prostituted themselves to false deities. Hence, God called them adulterers.

The word adultery can mean *illicit relationship*. Some words that describe *illicit* would be: immoral, improper, illegitimate. These words certainly describe what God is referring to as adultery. What they were doing was against everything He set before them—His laws that would keep them pure. Adultery defiled the holiness God demanded of them.

Go back to our key verse **2 Corinthians 11:2**. Keep reading in this passage. According to **verses 3-6**, how can we lose our pure devotion to Jesus Christ?

Clarify what an adulterer is according to **James 4:4**.

Think of a good friend. What makes this person such a good friend?

A friend is someone you feel close to. A friend is a person with whom you enjoy spending time. Friends are people we cherish—who are near to our hearts. James tells us that the world is not our friend because the world stands in opposition to God. Without a doubt, we can see that Satan rules the world we live in. God sets high standards, both ethically and morally, for His people. As we abide by these standards, we will remain pure. The world holds no such standards. Therefore, the world is not God's friend.

How do you see God's people becoming friends with the world?

Beloved One, do you see the importance in our message today? I believe the world is an alluring temptation. And if we are not careful, we can get entangled in its trap. It is easy to start off with God's mandate tucked inside our heart and our good intentions of following His ways. But Satan is there, dangling temptations before our eyes. I have watched people make terrible mistakes, simply because they have believed the grass is greener on the other side. Well, my friend, that is the enemy doing what he does best: deceiving God's people. And guess what? These well-intended people always find out that the grass is *not* greener on the other side. They compromised their beliefs, for what? For heartache, brokenness, and separation from God.

Look up **1 Kings 11:4**. What happened to Solomon as he became friends with other gods?

Now, listen to what I'm about to say. If we tend to sit on the fence, with one foot committed to righteous behavior and the other foot curious about the "so-called glamorous" world, then we can easily compromise our morals and, thus, become friends with the world. Believe this: when Satan shows up, he will be masked in magnificent colors and appealing garments. He knows what will catch our eye. He is a master. Solomon fell hard. We can too.

What word of advice does Barnabas offer the church at Antioch (**Acts 11:23**)?

How can this simple piece of advice help us to stay pure, undefiled by the world?

Idolatry! Compromise! Disregarding God's mandate! All of these are prevelant in the church today. Oh, how my heart is moved. These things may be subtle, but don't be fooled—they're there. I'm asking God to show me what things I have put in place of Him—what I have bowed to. We cannot present ourselves to Him as a virgin bride if we have become adulterers. In fact, Scripture indicates that the way to present ourselves pure to God is through a lifetime of partnership with Him.

Picture the day you stand before your Groom. His eyes are tender, beautiful. His face is filled with such love. You can tell He has longed for this day by the tender smile on His face and the way He looks into your eyes. Nothing is hidden from *His* eyes! He has patiently waited to see His beautiful Bride adorned in the most magnificent wedding garments. Close your eyes and watch Him move just a little closer. He takes the veil covering your face in His nail-scarred hands and lifts it over your head. Beloved, what will He find? Will He be presented with a virgin Bride who has kept herself pure for this moment—for her wedding day?

Ponder this. Write out your prayer to your Groom.

Day 2

KEEPING WATCH

Ask God to speak to your heart and show you His truth.

The key verse for today is **Matthew 24:42**. Please write out this verse.

Though I've written several other Bible studies, this one is especially near to my heart. For years, I have pondered the day when Jesus comes back for His Bride. I'm not sure why I've been thinking about it for so long—maybe because God has been preparing my heart for this project, this Bible study. Or perhaps because I can hardly contain myself when I think of the day God's people will be taken from this place—raptured from the earth. My mind often travels to that future day when we are all together, united with our Savior. Thinking about eternity keeps the hope alive inside me. My prayer is that you have begun to embrace this marvelous prophesy too, or that this Bible study has opened your eyes to see future things in a brighter light. Tim LaHaye writes, "God must have wanted His followers to learn Bible prophecy, because He dedicated almost 30 percent of His Scripture to it."[iv] Of course, many have already been fulfilled, but there are some prophesies still in the future, including the *Rapture of the Church* (**1 Thessalonians 4:16-17**) and the *Wedding of the Lamb* (**Revelation 19:7**).

Today we cover another ancient Jewish wedding custom—a custom that is crucial for believers to understand.

Ancient Custom #10: The bride watched and longed for the return of her groom.

After the groom finished preparing the house he would share with his bride, he would then return for her. However, the day or time of his arriving would remain a mystery to her. Yet, she was instructed to keep her eyes open and watch for her groom's return. She needed to be ready at any given moment. I picture this excited young girl laying her head on her pillow at night and wondering if it would be *this* night when her groom would show up. She must have dreamt of the moment he would arrive. How fast could she run? What would it feel like to fall into his arms? What would his face reveal? Most likely, her bags were packed and sitting by the door. Certainly, this expectant young bride wanted to be ready.

Read **Matthew 24:36-44** and summarize briefly.

Future prophesies cover a lot of ground. However, our previous passage is clearly referring to the *Rapture of the Church*. Matthew offers a good analogy—the flood that destroyed the earth. It took Noah approximately one hundred and twenty years to build the ark. During the construction, the people went about their daily lives, never considering that God was at work and something would one day come to pass—something that would affect the entire human race. The ark was a mammoth structure and occupied a large area of land. I wonder how many questions were asked of Noah. I imagine the people thought he was crazy. But Noah believed God. He was getting ready. What a shame for all those who had no regard for God. They couldn't be bothered. Regardless of the apathy though, God *did* what He said He would do. And it was only Noah and his family who were ready. Sadly, many believers are living like the people in Noah's day—they are not thinking about what's ahead. What God said would happen. Friend, let's not be like them. Let's model Noah's behavior and get ready. Remember, God *is* putting everything in place. He will come one day as He promised. We may not know when, but He *will* come.

The Bible often focuses on "staying awake." Jesus told the disciples, **"Watch and pray so that you will not fall into temptation" (Matthew 26:41)**. The psalmist prays, **"Open my eyes that I may see wonderful things in your law" (Psalm 119:18)**. Paul tells Timothy, **"Watch your life and doctrine closely" (I Timothy 4:16)**. We read in Proverbs, **"Blessed is the man who listens to me, watching daily at my doors, waiting at my doorway" (Proverbs 8:34)**. Hence, the Bible is clear: we are to keep our eyes open so that we will not be caught off guard. The only way to be ready is to watch, wait, and long for His return.

In relation to our topic today, there are two questions we need to answer: 1) *Why should we keep watching*; and 2) *How can we keep watch?*

Let's proceed with the first question:

Why should we keep watching?

1. It is commanded!

Look up the following passages and summarize your findings:

Mark 13:35-37:

Luke 12:35-40:

1 Thessalonians 5:6-7:

1 Corinthians 1:7:

Indeed, Jesus wants us to be ready. Perhaps Peter wouldn't have cut off the servant's ear— or denied his Savior—if he had stayed awake in the garden instead of sleeping. Had he only watched, things may have gone better for him. Maybe he would have understood the Father's plan. Staying awake might have made him ready. We are told to stay awake, to watch for His coming. This command is given for a reason. We should take heed and listen.

Now, for the second reason we should keep watching…

2. It will keep our passion alive!

What word did Jesus leave with us, according to **Matthew 28:18-20?**

The eternal torch was lit the moment Jesus lifted from this earth and the Church Age was born. The apostles and early believers carried that torch as far as they could, and then passed it to us. Now, it is our responsibility to bear that torch and share the Good News with others.

What is God's utmost desire, according to **2 Peter 3:9**?

That's right! God loves all mankind and does not want anyone to suffer eternal condemnation. He longs for everyone to be with Him in glory. We don't have time to cover the end-time chronology here, but there are reputable scholars who believe the Rapture of the Church will likely precede the seven-year tribulation period. If you study John's Revelation, you can shape your own interpretation, but I'm certain of one important thing: you and I do not want any of our loved ones, friends or acquaintances to have to endure the tribulation period. These seven years will be horrendous, especially for those who come to know Christ during this time. And you must agree with me that the more passion we have for something, the more we will try to influence people. There is not a greater passion to have than for the Gospel of Jesus Christ. By keeping our eyes open and focused on Jesus' return, a deeper passion will be ignited in us to share the truth of salvation with everyone we meet. Hence, we will be stronger witnesses for the cause of Christ.

Now, let's quickly cover the second question:

How can we keep watch?

1. Stay informed!

While we do not know when our Groom will return for His Bride, God did give us enough information to keep us informed. In our next two lessons, we will observe some of the prophetic passages that shed more light on what to look for as the end approaches. However, there are some very good resources in Christian bookstores that can further open up end-time prophesies. Many of these authors have spent years researching prophetic happenings. Of course, there are also many false prophets, so we need to choose carefully. Ask your pastor, your mentor, or someone you trust to give you a list of reputable authors and/or resource materials. One author I respect is Tim LaHaye. He has written numerous books on the end-times. Hopefully, this Bible study will also help you stay informed.

Here's the second way we can keep watch…

2. Look for the signs!

Look up **Matthew 24:3**. What questions did the disciples ask Jesus?

After the disciples proposed these questions, Jesus spent considerable time listing some end-time signs—signs that will be present *just* prior to His return. We will cover these signs in our next two lessons, but I want to encourage you to study the signs. Then look around. What do you see? While every generation has believed it was their generation to see the return of Christ, the signs have never been stronger than for *this* generation. We must not bury our heads in the sand like many believers. Doubters are filling the church. They simply cannot believe Christ's return could be soon because it seems we have been waiting a long time. God *will* send His Son to retrieve His Bride, and we must be ready.

What advice does **Proverbs 4:20-27** offer?

Relate these words of wisdom from Proverbs to "keeping watch." What is speaking to your heart?

Day 3

SIGNS OF THE TIMES – PART 1

Ask God to speak to your heart and show you His truth.

The key verse for today is **Matthew 24:33**. Please write out this verse.

What a blessing that the disciples asked Jesus, **"When will this happen, and what will be the sign of your coming and of the end of the age" (Matthew 24:3)**? Jesus then answered their questions. In addition to what Jesus said, other New Testament passages also record certain details about the end days. What's important to note is the Bible is complete with what we need to know about the end days and the specific signs to look for. At the very end of the Bible we read, **"If anyone adds anything to them, God will add to him the plagues described in this book. And if anyone takes words away from this book of prophecy, God will take away from him his share in the tree of life and in the holy city, which are described in this book" (Revelation 22:18-19)**.

The next two days we will investigate some of these signs—the signs that will prevail before Jesus returns. Of course, end-time prophesy is far more extensive than what we have time for, but we will try to cover the most important aspects with as much detail as possible. Then it's important that you take what you learn and look around, asking yourself if you see these signs prevalent in our world today. We might agree that these end-time elements have been a part of our world for centuries, but are they escalating? The rapid succession of these biblical truths is critical to understanding how close we might be to Jesus' return.

Let's begin by observing a key passage: **Matthew 24:4-14**. List every sign mentioned.

What does **Matthew 24:32-35** tell us about these signs?

Please follow along as we key in on each of the signs mentioned in this passage. What specifics does the Bible give" What are some of those things to look for?

- **False prophets (Matthew 24:4-5)!**

False prophets crept into the body of Christ as far back as the first century, but during the end days, there will be many people bringing shame upon the kingdom of God as they twist the Word for their own gain. The topic of false prophets is addressed throughout the New Testament. Together, let's look at two prevailing features about these counterfeit prophets.

False prophets are...

Deceivers!

Jesus said it best: **"Watch out that no one deceives you. For many will come in my name, claiming, 'I am the Christ,' and will deceive many" (Matthew 24:4-5)**. What do you learn about these deceivers from the following verses?

Romans 16:18:

Ephesians 5:6:

Colossians 2:4:

One definition for *deceive* is: "to mislead by a false appearance."[v] Jesus tells us that even the "elect" will be deceived (**Matthew 24:24**). We might ask ourselves, "How is that possible?" Well, my friend, these charismatic deceivers know the Word of God and they teach with passion and enthusiasm. Some have large followings. They twist the Word of God, they eliminate parts of Scripture, and they do not teach the full gospel. They are persuasive! And they have succeeded in misleading thousands, *even* believers.

The Apostle Paul exposed the deceivers to the Galatian church (**Galatians 1:6-7**). From this passage, what does Paul tell us about false teachers?

Sadly, many flock to hear these alluring preachers spew lies. Perhaps they are drawn because there is no accountability for their sin. Paul said to Timothy, **"For the time will come when men will**

not put up with sound doctrine. Instead, to suit their own desires, they will gather around them a great number of teachers to say what their itching ears want to hear. They will turn their ears away from the truth and turn aside to myths" (2 Timothy 4:3-4). Friends, this time has come! Not only are these false prophets deceptive, but it's so subtle many do not recognize the fabrications.

What sound advice is given in **1 Thessalonians 5:21-22** to help us *pick out* a false prophet? How can we be protected from being led astray?

That's right! You can recognize a false prophet by testing their doctrine against the doctrine of the Bible. If what they say does not line up with Scripture, then don't listen. Not long ago many people were led astray by a preacher who predicted Jesus would come back on a certain day. Believing in his lies, some of his followers sold everything they owned. Jesus clearly tells us that **"no one knows about that day or hour, not even the angels in heaven, nor the Son, but only the Father" (Matthew 24:36).** If these agreeable people would have only tested this preacher's prophesy against the Bible's prophesy, they may not have followed. Another well-known preacher stands before his congregation of thousands week after week and never discusses sin. He is more concerned with popularity than holding to the absolute truth of God's Word. My friend, this is simply not the whole gospel. Jesus confronted people with their sin issues. Sin is bondage! And we cannot experience true freedom without confronting our sin and then making ourselves right with Christ. Consequently, our world is full of false prophets who are leading multitudes astray. Satan is on a warpath and continues, at an alarming rate, to lure many people away from the truth of God's Word and into his web of counterfeit lies. Jesus and the New Testament writers often discussed these dangerous deceivers— deceivers who will multiply during the end days. Therefore, we *should* pay attention.

False prophets are also…

Destructive!

What does Peter tell us about false prophets in **2 Peter 2:1-3**?

Describe false prophets using **Philippians 3:18-19** and **Colossians 2:4**.

Precious One, Scripture holds enough information about these destructive prophets that help believers identify who they are. So, don't be fooled! They are some of Satan's strongest ambassadors. Thus, they are *not* working for God. In fact, they have learned deception from the master deceiver himself. These phony preachers continue to mislead people—even the elect— with destructive heresy. Anyone who chooses to follow will encounter disastrous results The Bible tells us that in the end days, false prophets will increase. Have you observed any false teachers yet? Explain based on what you have learned about them.

Now, let's move forward to several other end-time features:

• **Wars and rumors of wars (Matthew 24:6-7)!**

Tim LaHaye says, "The twentieth century has been far bloodier than any century that preceded it. Far more people have died in wars during the past hundred years than in all the centuries before. And wars just keep proliferating."[vi] In addition, there is a constant threat of increased terrorism, and countries that promise to make good on launching weapons of mass destruction. Indeed, this end-time sign is no doubt prevalent today.

- **Famines (Matthew 24:7)!**

Whether we see it or not, it's true that a large number of the earth's population is suffering from famine—millions of people go to bed hungry at night. After my friend returned from her recent trip to Haiti, she commented how mortified she was seeing the horrible malnourishment of the Haitian people. Surely, this is one end-time sign that has increased in the last century.

- **Earthquakes (Matthew 24:7)!**

Earthquakes are one of God's most powerful disasters the earth has confronted. When God wants to make a statement, He often chooses earthquakes to do it. An earthquake reminds us that He is still God, He's still seated on the throne, and He's still in control. An earthquake also reminds us that this is God's earth and He can do what He wants. Biblically speaking, earthquakes have been used by God for centuries. Based on the following passages, what do you learn about each act of God?

Matthew 27:50-54:

Matthew 28:1-2:

Acts 4:23-31:

Acts 16:24-28:

When God chooses to make Himself and His purposes known, He *always* does it with power and authority. I don't think there is a more compelling way for God to reveal His dominion and authority than through earthquakes. I do not think the earthquake following Jesus' death was felt *only* in Jerusalem. No, I believe the whole earth—inhabited or not—was forcefully moved the day Jesus took His last breath and God's great redemptive plan fulfilled. With the earth rumbling beneath their feet, even the centurion and those with him recognized Jesus as the Son of God (**Matthew 27:54**). Then, *just* two days later, God shook the earth again to bring forth His Son back from the dead. The early believers also experienced the earth move on at least two separate occasions. Consequently, God has used earthquakes many times to accomplish His greater purposes and/or to make His voice heard.

Summarize **Ezekiel 38:17-23**.

Earthquakes are also signs of judgment. Theologians agree that this prophesy in Ezekiel is yet to take place. What we *do* learn from this passage is that on this day, an army will come and overwhelm Israel. God will then execute a great earthquake to judge those who have no regard for Him, and to also protect His country. Everything in its wake will be destroyed.

For centuries, God has been speaking through earthquakes. It is His way of declaring to the world His sovereignty, His dominion. We read that earthquakes will be an end-time sign (**Matthew 24:8**). The earthquakes referred to in **Matthew 24:8** are warning signs—signs that God will bring judgment upon this earth. We read in John's Revelation, **"Since you have kept my command to endure patiently, I will also keep you from the hour of trial that is going to come upon the whole world to test those who live on this earth" (Revelation 3:10)**. Many scholars believe this verse promises that the Church will be raptured before the seven-year tribulation period begins. Regardless, we need to know that earthquakes are a powerful sign that the end days are upon us. Studies have shown that the number of earthquakes has increased *greatly* in this last century and they are continuing at an accelerated rate. So, my friend, let's pay attention.

What is God speaking to you about today?

Day 4

SIGNS OF THE TIMES – PART 2

Ask God to speak to your heart and show you His truth.

The key verse for today is **2 Timothy 3:1**. Please write out this verse.

I trust you are hanging in there with me. It's to our advantage that we observe these end-time signs closely. The detailed messages Jesus gave regarding the signs indicate their importance, and the Bible reminds us we are to keep our eyes open so we will be ready. My dad believed *ours* is the chosen generation for the Rapture. After studying the signs, researching our world today, and looking around, I firmly agree. It's important you hear what I have to say *now*. Believers— those who have received Jesus Christ as their Savior—have no reason to fear the future. God loves His people immeasurably, and He promises to protect us from His greatest wrath (**Revelation 3:10**). However, knowing the end is swiftly approaching should make us stronger witnesses for Jesus Christ.

In our previous lesson, we looked at some end-time signs: false prophets, wars and rumors of wars, famines, and earthquakes. Today, we'll examine two further signs: *persecution* and *godlessness*. At the conclusion of our lesson, I believe you and I will agree that these two signs are rampant in today's world, and even in our own country.

We need to return to our Matthew passage. Read **Matthew 24:9** and **12**. Write down what you read about the end times.

From these verses, there are two signs popping up in the end days:

- **Persecution!**

Read **John 15:18-21**, and answer the following questions:

What is the world's response to Christians?

What will happen to Christians and why?

Jesus tells us that Satan is the **"prince of this world" (John 16:11)**. In other words, the earth is his domain. For this reason, the world—the place we live—is in opposition to Jesus. And because Christians represent Jesus, Satan's greatest enemy, they will be persecuted just as He was. We should not be surprised Christians are the most targeted group in the world—Jesus said this would happen. And in the end days, persecution of Christians will increase. Just because the media rarely discusses world persecution of Christians does not mean it's not happening. In fact, the opposite is true. Just today, I ran across two headlines: "Christians More Persecuted Today Than at any Time" and "Religious Persecution on the Rise."

Here are some staggering statistics found on one website:[vii]

- In Indonesia from 1998-2003, 10,000 Christians were murdered and 1,000 homes burned down.

- In India in 2008, more than 100 Christians murdered and 50,000 displaced.

- In Nigeria in 2010, 500 Christians slaughtered, mostly women and children.

- Historically, 70 million people have been killed for their Christian faith.

(Over 45 million in the 20th century)

Here are a few headlines throughout the world in recent weeks:

- Religious Minorities Subject to Cruel Treatment.

- Chinese House Church Repeatedly Targeted for Persecution. Members Detained and Sent to Labor Camp.

- Pakistani Woman Charged with Blasphemy for Refusing Islam.

- India Militants Attacked Prayer Meeting, Pastors.

- Iranian Pastor Sentenced to Death.

- Persecuted Church in Beijing Reports Sunday Morning Arrests.

- Another Church in Jos, Nigeria Hit by Suicide Bombing.

- Lands Drenched in Innocent Blood: Boko Haram Declares War Against Christians.

- North Korea: Seven Underground Churches Raided.

While it is true other countries see far more Christian persecution than the United States, it is certainly growing in our country. Here are a few recent headlines in the United States:

- American Girl, 14, Gets Death Threats for Defending Marriage.

- Atheist Group Launches Another Assault on Jesus Statue.

- Teachers Not Allowed to Bow Heads, Pray Silently by School Board.

- Atheists Want Cross Removed From September 11th Memorial.

Without a doubt, Jesus' prophesy is abounding. Persecution, especially in the United States, is gaining momentum. For instance, God—or the mention of God—is being eliminated in text books, government speeches, laws, and across college campuses. Those who stand up for biblical truth are often ostracized and mocked. Our country was founded on God's Word, but in the last few decades, we've noticed a rapid decline in biblical principles—Christian freedoms are slowly being taken from us. One conservative Christian commentator is convinced the 21st century Church will be forced to do exactly as the early Church: worship underground.

As an optional exercise, you may want to "Google" Christian persecution. Write down your findings on a separate sheet of paper.

Do you find Christian persecution on the rise? Give some examples.

What does Paul tell us about persecution in **2 Timothy 3:12-13**?

Read further in this passage. What is required of us according to **2 Timothy 3:14-17**?

What hopeful words can be found in **Matthew 5:11-12**?

Does this help you during these end days? How?

Now, let's cover our last end-time sign:

- **Godlessness!**

Three words that would best describe *godlessness* are: wicked, evil, sinful. In my lifetime, I've witnessed godlessness abound. Wicked behavior has certainly increased in the last couple decades. The following passages shed light on how godlessness will look in the end days. Summarize your findings.

2 Timothy 3:1-9:

Galatians 5:19-21:

Now, add any further features by observing **Romans 1:24-31**.

You must agree that most—or all of these things—have exploded within the last couple decades. On Day 3, we discussed two ways to keep watch: 1) Stay informed; and 2) Look for the signs. Let's practice. Scan over the list. Next to each item, write out how you've witnessed it change within the last two decades — or the last several years. How has it declined morally? How has it increased? You can visit websites like—Focus on the Family, Family Research Council, and Wallbuilders—to answer more effectively. Use additional paper if needed.

Marriage:

Morals and values:

Alternative lifestyles:

Violence:

Public school education:

Entertainment:

Media:

Government:

The Bible / Christianity:

The Church:

Of course, there are many more things we could add to this list. I imagine we have all noticed that the fiber of our country has deteriorated and godlessness has risen quickly in this century alone. Beloved, let's keep our eyes focused on these signs the Bible tells us represent the end days.

Day 5

STAYING STRONG

Ask God to speak to your heart and show you His truth.

The key verse for today is **Isaiah 35:4**. Please write out this verse.

Before we proceed with today's topic, we need to examine two more end-time signs. We find them in one Old Testament verse. Look up **Daniel 12:4** and write down what they are.

As we live in the age of air travel, computers, the Internet, and phenomenal medical breakthroughs, we can see with certainty these end-time signs are indeed increasing in this 21st century. How have you seen *travel* and *knowledge* increase within the last few decades? How?

Are your eyes getting wider as we discuss these biblical facts relating to the end days? I confess I am disappointed with the apathy I see in the Church today. I've heard believers say, "For centuries, people have believed it was *their* generation to see the end. Earthquakes, false prophets, famines, and godlessness have been a part of every past century." While there is a lot of truth to these statements, let me remind you these things are increasing by insurmountable numbers. Therefore, let's not maintain the same indifferent attitude as many 21st century believers. Keep your eyes opened as Jesus said, and stay focused on God's eternal Word. By doing these things, you will then be able to help others get ready too.

It's true we are living in perilous times, but there is no reason to be afraid. These end-time signs were recorded to help us be ready when our Bridegroom returns for His Bride. These signs also remind us we need to stay strong as the end approaches. One thing is sure: there are some believers in our Christian circles who are weaker than others. The weaker Christians are those who have not yet grown to maturity in their faith—their understanding of God's Word is still developing. Though they love Jesus and are learning to trust in His Word, they may be a little more fearful when the topic of the end days is discussed. This is when the mature believer can help the weaker brother or sister find strength. But, seasoned believers *need* to be strong themselves.

What useful advice did the Apostle Paul leave with Timothy in **2 Timothy 2:1**?

There's strong evidence to suggest that Paul's second letter to Timothy was his last. We read in **2 Timothy 4:7, "I have fought the good fight, I have finished the race."** As Paul was focused on his *own* impending death, it makes sense he encouraged Timothy to stay strong. Paul knew the days ahead for Timothy would be difficult, so he was sure to point out the importance of remaining strong. What great counsel for today's believers! We surely don't know what the days ahead will be like for God's chosen people. I pray that today's lesson will guide us in our endeavor to stay strong.

According to **Ephesians 6:10**, where does our strength come from?

Staying strong during these uncertain days is possible, Precious One, but our strength can *only* be found in God. Allow me to present four ways to help us remain strong.

1. Stay true to the Word of God!

What did God tell the new leader of His people, according to **Joshua 1:6-9**?

Review this passage again and draw your own comparisons between *strength* and *God's Word*.

After Moses died, God appointed Joshua as His new leader, the one who would lead the nation from the wilderness—the place they had called home for forty years—into their new land. However, the work would not be easy. With new things come new challenges. Moses had been a beloved leader. The people of Israel were often rebellious and worldly. Instead of Joshua going to Moses for advice, the people would *now* turn to him. What if he was a disappointment? What if the people did not like their new leader? Was he qualified to take over? What if he failed God? As Joshua looked to the future, perhaps questions like these haunted him.

But God did not abandon Joshua. In fact, He offered him some *great* advice. Basically He said, "Joshua, keep My Word before you.

Don't be swayed by what others say, and do not let your heart be deceived by people who try to lead you astray. No! When you need courage, open My powerful Book. When you're afraid, go to My Word for strength. When you come under attack, My Word will fight for you. Joshua, do not drift from the Word, and don't rely on your own strength. Meditate on this Book of the Law day and night. This is all you need to succeed as My new leader."

Compare **1 John 2:14** with the advice given to Joshua.

How does this advice help you as you look to the future? How will you put it to practice in your life?

2. Put on the full armor of God!

What admonition does Paul propose for strength in **Ephesians 6:10-11**?

What does the full armor of God do for us according to **Ephesians 6:11-13**?

What similarities do you find between these things in **Ephesians 6:11-13** and the end days?

We don't have time to examine each armor piece, but glance through the list (**Ephesians 6:14-18**) and write down ways you can apply the armor pieces to your life.

God has equipped us with everything we need for strength during these uncertain days. As a Roman soldier would *never* venture into battle unprotected—each piece of armor was in place—we have been given divinely crafted armor for the spiritual battle before us. It can protect us against the fiercest enemies. Nonetheless, we need to become adept at using the armor.

3. Work hard!

Summarize **2 Timothy 2:1-6**.

This passage includes the following instructions:

- **Teach others what we have been taught (verse 2);**
- **Endure hardship (verse 3);**
- **Compete according to the rules (verse 5).**

What is the result of dedicated effort, according to **verse 6**?

Working hard is always a good thing, but working hard for God's kingdom reaps eternal benefits. Pouring ourselves into God's work is a sure way to stay strong during these difficult days. However, **2 Timothy 2:5** reminds us it's important to work according to God's ways, not ours. Any other way to work will ultimately be a waste of our time, and a loss of rewards (**1 Corinthians 3:15**).

4. Keep our eyes on the future!

Read **Hebrews 11:8-16**. What was the focus of some of our early forefathers?

Now, recap **Hebrews 11:35-40**.

Certainly, we can never imagine the difficulties the Old Testament saints and early believers endured. In the early Church, persecution abounded, Christians were horribly mistreated, and some suffered slow and agonizing deaths. The writer of Hebrews gives us small glimpses into the pain many believers faced at the hands of their enemies. The question then becomes: How *did* they stay strong for their families—their children—in the midst of such dreadful conditions? I believe our passage in Hebrews tells us how—they kept their eyes on their *promised* future, their inheritance awaiting them. What a valuable reminder for each of us, especially as we see more and more of God's predictions come to pass.

Do you find yourself teetering on the "weak" side or the "strong" side? Ponder this question, and then answer honestly. Explain your answer.

Review today's lesson. Choose one of the four points and explain how you can put it into practice to help you remain strong during these days.

Oh, my dear friend. I'm thrilled you are still with me. I admit this is the hardest Bible study I've written. But the most exciting study, too. I enjoy focusing on the horizon. I cannot wait for the day I fall into the arms of my Savior and feel His tender arms wrapped around me. I cannot wait to look into His eyes and hear the sound of His voice, especially as He speaks my name. I hope you are getting more excited too.

I pray you enjoyed this portion of my bible study. To order the complete study of "The Bride of Christ ~ Becoming Rapture Ready," visit www.solidtruthministries.com or www.amazon.com.

ABOUT SHERYL

There is nothing that gives me greater joy than to watch God open up peoples' hearts to the truth of His Word. Words cannot describe the joy in my heart every time I hear what God is doing in the lives of His people through one of our Bible studies. Sometimes I think I can hear heaven's hosts shouting "Halleluiah."

While I have been writing and teaching Bible studies for years, this Bible study has my heart soaring high. I believe that every study I've written so far, has only prepared me for this eternal project. No doubt, it is driven by the Holy Spirit and anointed by God. Please stay in touch with me and let me know how this study impacted your life.

Thank you for your partnership.

In Him,

Sheryl

Sheryl Pellatiro is an active Bible study teacher, author, and speaker. Her website hosts many of her Bible teachings. She would love to hear from you: Sheryl@solidtruthministries.com.

ABOUT THE AUTHOR

Rosemary Fisher is a wife, mother, author and national conference speaker. She has been featured on CBN "700 Club", "Bridges Show", "Freedom Today", "Atlanta LIVE" and numerous television and radio programs around the country.

Rosemary's latest book, **Broken Hearts Have NO Color** is available at www.Amazon.com or major bookstores.

To find out more about Rosemary, her speaking ministry and Bride of Christ Conferences, visit www.rosemaryfisher.com

Rosemary's books are available in special quantity discounts when purchased in bulk by corporations, organizations and special –interest groups. Custom imprinting or excerpting can also be done to fit special needs. For information and pricing, please email rosemary@rosemaryfisher.com

But seek first his kingdom and his righteousness, and all these things will be given to you as well.

Matthew 6:33

[i] Bonus Stories provided from Broken Hearts Have No Color by Rosemary Fisher

[ii] "From *Holiness: The Heart God Purifies*, ©2004, 2005 by Nancy Leigh DeMoss. Used with permission of Moody Publishers. All rights reserved."

[iii] (*http://www.facingforever.org/downloads/lost_in_church.pdf*)

[iv] Tim LaHaye, *Are we Living in the End Times* (Illinois: Tyndale House Publishers, 1999), 3.
[v] http://dictionary.reference.com/browse/deceive?s=t

[vi] Tim LaHaye, *Are we Living in the End Times* (Illinois: Tyndale House Publishers, 1999), 38.

[vii] http://www.persecution.org/awareness/

42274072R00073

Made in the USA
Middletown, DE
06 April 2017